Better Homes and Gardens.

CHRISTMAS
FROM THE HEART.

Volume 18

Meredith® Books
Des Moines, Iowa

Better Homes and Gardens.
CHRISTMAS
FROM THE HEART.

Creative Director: Brenda Drake Lesch
Contributing Editor: Carol Field Dahlstrom
Contributing Food Editors: Winifred Moranville, Joyce Trollope
Contributing Designer: Angie Haupert Hoogensen
Editorial Assistant: Cathy Celsi
Book Production Manager: Mark Weaver
Contributing Copy Editor: Carol DeMasters
Contributing Proofreaders: Laura DeBoer, Judith Stern
  Friedman, Karen Grossman
Contributing Photographer: Jay Wilde
Contributing Technical Illustrator: Chris Neubauer
  Graphics, Inc.
Contributing Project Designers: Judy Bailey, Kristin Detrick,
  Barb Jones, Lynn Jones, Janet Petersma, Ann E. Smith,
  Jan Temeyer
Contributing Recipe Development: David Feder, R.D.
Test Kitchen Director: Lynn Blanchard
Test Kitchen Product Supervisor: Jill Moberly
Test Kitchen Culinary Specialists: Marilyn Cornelius, Juliana
  Hale, Maryellyn Krantz, Colleen Weeden, Lori Wilson
Test Kitchen Nutrition Specialists: Elizabeth Burt, R.D., L.D.;
  Laura Marzen, R.D., L.D.

Meredith® Books
Editor in Chief, Creative Collection: Deborah Gore Ohrn
Managing Editor: Kathleen Armentrout
Brand Manager: Mark Mooberry
Copy Chief: Doug Kouma
Senior Copy Editors: Kevin Cox, Jennifer Speer Ramundt,
  Elizabeth Keest Sedrel
Assistant Copy Editor: Metta Cederdahl
Proofreader: Joleen Ross

Executive Director, Sales: Ken Zagor
Director, Operations: George A. Susral
Business Director: Janice Croat

Vice President and General Manager, SIP: Jeff Myers

***Better Homes and Gardens®* Magazine**
Editor in Chief: Gayle Goodson Butler

Meredith Publishing Group
President: Jack Griffin
President, *Better Homes and Gardens®*: Andy Sareyan
Vice President, Corporate Solutions: Michael Brownstein
Vice President, Manufacturing: Bruce Heston
Vice President, Consumer Marketing: David Ball
Director, Creative Services: Grover Kirkman
Consumer Product Marketing Director: Steve Swanson
Consumer Product Marketing Manager: Wendy Merical
Business Director: Jim Leonard

Meredith Corporation
Chairman of the Board: William T. Kerr
President and Chief Executive Officer: Stephen M. Lacy

In Memoriam: E.T. Meredith III (1933–2003)

Our seal assures you that every recipe in
Christmas from the Heart 2009 has been tested
in the Better Homes and Gardens® Test Kitchen.
This means that each recipe is practical and
reliable, and meets our high standards of taste
appeal. We guarantee your satisfaction with
this book for as long as you own it.

Better Homes and Gardens®

CHRISTMAS
FROM THE HEART®

contents

Let the Christmas tree be the center of attention with handmade ornaments and garlands that will be treasured forever.

oh. christmas
tree

Combine beautifully shaped hydrangeas and a dusting of glitter to create **Sparkling Hydrangeas**, *above*. Then tuck them into an evergreen tree wherever you want a touch of elegance. Add pink jeweled balls, quick-to-make trims using purchased stickers, garlands of fresh cranberries and limes, and clusters of shiny Christmas balls to make a **Christmas Tree in Pink and Green**, *opposite*. Instructions begin on page 16. Turn the page for a closeup look at the lovely collection of ornaments and garland that adorn this holiday tree.

Just for fun, make **3-D Paper Packages**, *top left*, using pretty scrapbook papers and a jingle bell. For a quick idea with an evergreen theme, wrap a **Rickrack Package**, *bottom left*.

For a fresh look and wonderful scent, gather the whole family together to help string a **Cranberry Garland**, *opposite top*, to encircle your evergreen tree. Choose stickers from a local scrapbooking store and create **Quick Stickered Trims**, *opposite top right*, in colors to match your holiday theme. So quick to make, yet so elegant, **Jeweled in Pink Trims**, *opposite bottom*, add a special shimmering sparkle to the tree. Instructions, pages 16–17.

Assorted fabric scraps turn into **Pretty Beaded Motifs**, *below*, when they are embellished with colorful beads and wire. Choose your favorite holiday motif and beads that make them sparkle.

Buttons, buttons, and more buttons are all it takes to make a **Holiday Button Tree**, *opposite*. Use new purchased buttons or vintage buttons to make your tree one-of-a-kind. Display as a centerpiece or on a mantel. Instructions are on pages 17–19.

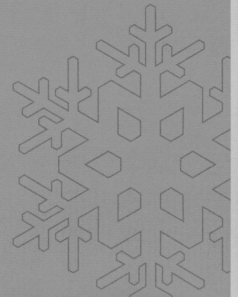

Get the kids involved in making trims by creating their own **Namesake Ornament**, *opposite top*. Give a purchased trim personality with simple alphabet stickers. Brighten up the tree in no time with **Sparkling Geometric Trims**, *opposite,* using orange ornaments, double-sided tape, and a little glitter.

Gather small cardboard jewelry boxes and wrap them to make a **Stacked Package Trim**, *above*. Glue the boxes together and add a bow topper. Instructions are on pages 19–20.

Layer inexpensive felt in the colors that you favor to create a set of **Felt Cutouts**, *opposite*. Then add some decorative stitches to complete the pretty and soft trims.

Spell out your joy and add some jewels or just use pretty jewels and glitter to make **Christmas Green Trims**, *above*. Instructions are on pages 20–21.

Sparkling Hydrangeas
Shown on page 6

WHAT YOU NEED
Purchased dried or artificial hydrangeas
Wire cutters
Crafts glue
Water
Paintbrush
Fine light green glitter

HERE'S HOW
Lay the hydrangeas on a covered surface
and clip off the heads to the desired
length. Mix equal parts of glue and water
and brush on the flower head using a
paintbrush. Sprinkle with glitter. Shake
off excess. Allow to dry.

3-D Paper Packages
Shown on page 8

WHAT YOU NEED
Tracing paper or copier
Pencil
Scissors
2-sided scrapbook paper in desired
    patterns and colors
Paper punch
1 yard ½-inch wide ribbon
Fine wire
8 inches narrow ribbon
Red jingle bell

HERE'S HOW
1. Copy or trace the pattern, *below*.
Transfer to the scrapbook paper and cut
out. Cut the slits in the pieces. Punch
holes at the top and bottom of the
package shape. Slide the two pieces of
paper together.
2. Make a bow with the ½-inch-wide
ribbon and wire it to the top of the paper
package using the punched holes to
secure. Add the narrow ribbon through
the hole for a hanger. Thread the bell
onto the wire and attach through the
holes at the bottom of the package.

Rickrack Package
Shown on page 8

WHAT YOU NEED
Pencil
Package wrapped in solid color paper
Lengths of rickrack
Scissors
Crafts glue
Clear tape
Tree-shape stickers

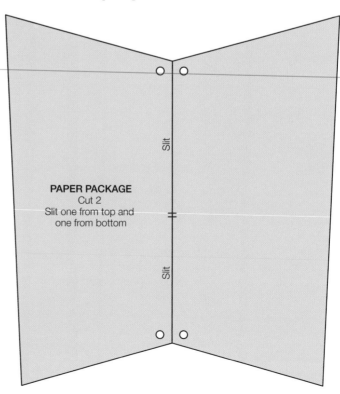

Slit

Slit

PAPER PACKAGE
Cut 2
Slit one from top and
one from bottom

HERE'S HOW

With a pencil mark where the rickrack will be placed on the package. Cut the rickrack to fit the package and glue in place. Put a piece of tape over where the rickrack ends in the back to secure. Place stickers in a row above the rickrack.

Cranberry Garland

Shown on page 9

WHAT YOU NEED

Fresh cranberries
Fresh limes
Sharp knife
Large needle
Waxed dental floss

HERE'S HOW

Wash the cranberries and the limes. Slice the limes into thin slices. Set aside. Thread the needle with the floss. Start stringing the cranberries, leaving at least 12 inches of floss for tying to the tree. Secure the first cranberry on the floss by putting the needle through twice making a knot. Continue threading the cranberries and limes until desired length is achieved. Tie the knot at the end leaving enough floss for tying to the tree. **Note:** Cranberries and limes will stay fresh looking for days and then will dry nicely on the tree for up to three weeks.

Quick Stickered Trims

Shown on page 9

WHAT YOU NEED

Large purchased matte-finish ball ornament
Small purchased stickers in desired shapes
Wood orange stick
Narrow ribbon

HERE'S HOW

Be sure the ball is clean and dry. Decide on the placement of the stickers. Carefully peel off the stickers and place where desired. Use the orange stick to smooth the stickers to the ball. Place a ribbon at the top of the ornament and tie a bow if desired.

Jeweled in Pink Trims

Shown on page 9

WHAT YOU NEED

Purchased matte-finish pink ornament
Small tumbler or drinking glass
Crafts glue
Fine pink glitter
Pink jewels

HERE'S HOW

Set the ornament in the tumbler. Make lines of glue starting from the top of the ornament. Sprinkle the glitter over the glue. Add a jewel at the end of the glittered glue line. Allow to dry.

Pretty Beaded Motifs

Shown on page 10

WHAT YOU NEED

Tracing paper
Pencil
Scissors
Assorted fabric scraps
Scrap iron-on stabilizer, such as Pellon brand Peltex #72, double-sided fusible ultrafirm stabilizer
Iridescent glitter
24-gauge gold craft wire
Fabric glue
White glue
Assorted glass beads
9-mm gold jingle bells

oh christmas tree

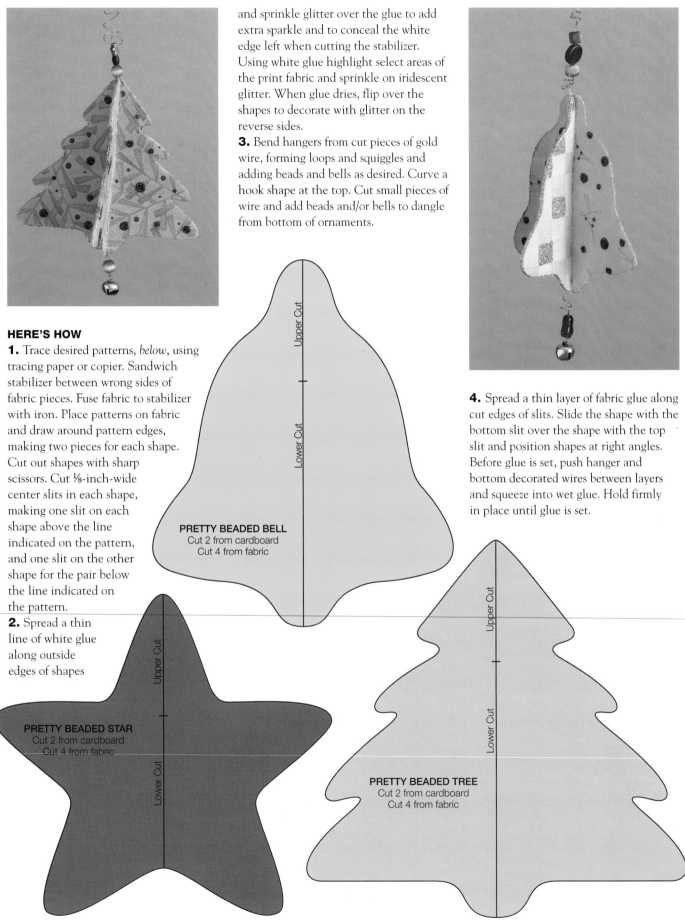

and sprinkle glitter over the glue to add extra sparkle and to conceal the white edge left when cutting the stabilizer. Using white glue highlight select areas of the print fabric and sprinkle on iridescent glitter. When glue dries, flip over the shapes to decorate with glitter on the reverse sides.

3. Bend hangers from cut pieces of gold wire, forming loops and squiggles and adding beads and bells as desired. Curve a hook shape at the top. Cut small pieces of wire and add beads and/or bells to dangle from bottom of ornaments.

HERE'S HOW

1. Trace desired patterns, *below*, using tracing paper or copier. Sandwich stabilizer between wrong sides of fabric pieces. Fuse fabric to stabilizer with iron. Place patterns on fabric and draw around pattern edges, making two pieces for each shape. Cut out shapes with sharp scissors. Cut ⅛-inch-wide center slits in each shape, making one slit on each shape above the line indicated on the pattern, and one slit on the other shape for the pair below the line indicated on the pattern.

2. Spread a thin line of white glue along outside edges of shapes

4. Spread a thin layer of fabric glue along cut edges of slits. Slide the shape with the bottom slit over the shape with the top slit and position shapes at right angles. Before glue is set, push hanger and bottom decorated wires between layers and squeeze into wet glue. Hold firmly in place until glue is set.

Upper Cut

Lower Cut

PRETTY BEADED BELL
Cut 2 from cardboard
Cut 4 from fabric

Upper Cut

Lower Cut

PRETTY BEADED STAR
Cut 2 from cardboard
Cut 4 from fabric

Upper Cut

Lower Cut

PRETTY BEADED TREE
Cut 2 from cardboard
Cut 4 from fabric

buttons randomly around the lower portion of the tree. (If desired, dip the pin shaft into glue before inserting into the cone.) Layer some contrasting smaller buttons onto the large buttons. As you are working, check your tree for balance of color/button size and adjust as necessary. Continue by placing medium buttons of contrasting colors adjacent to the large buttons.

3. Fill in the gaps between the larger buttons with the smallest buttons. Add buttons until no foam cone is visible. Use small buttons at the top of the tree. Add star or other ornament to the top of the tree.

Namesake Ornament
Shown on page 12

WHAT YOU NEED
Glass or plastic ornaments
Sticker letters
Ribbon for hanging loops

HERE'S HOW
Choose ornaments with horizontal stripes (solid-color ornaments will work, too). Make a list of the names or words you want to add to the ornaments. Select adhesive letters in a size that will enable you to fit the names or words onto the ornaments. Press the letters onto the ornaments, keeping the letters aligned at the bottom. Add a ribbon for hanging.

Sparkling Geometric Trims
Shown on page 12

WHAT YOU NEED
Purchased Christmas ornaments
Double-sided tape
Scissors
Orange or gold glitter
Narrow ribbon (optional)

HERE'S HOW
Be sure ornament is clean and dry. Use scissors to cut thin pieces of tape, squares of tape, or other geometric shapes. Carefully adhere the shapes to ornament. Peel off other side of tape. Dust with glitter. Add a ribbon for hanging.

Holiday Button Tree
Shown on page 11

WHAT YOU NEED
12-inch foam cone such, as
    Styrofoam cone
250+ buttons in a variety of sizes
    and colors
250+ pins with large heads
White crafts glue (optional)
Star or other ornament for the top
    of the tree

HERE'S HOW
1. Select a color scheme for the tree. Purchase buttons in the color scheme in a variety of sizes (small, medium, and large) or use antique buttons. Sort the buttons by size and color.

2. Beginning with the largest buttons, insert a pin into a button hole and pin the button to the cone. Place the largest

oh christmas tree

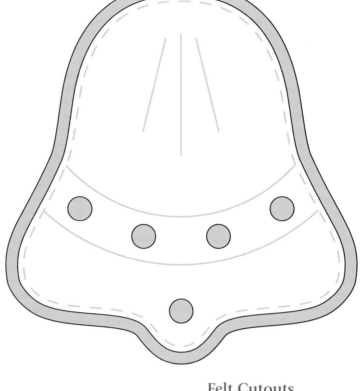

Stacked Package Trim

Shown on page 13

WHAT YOU NEED

Three small boxes in graduated sizes,
    such as jewelry boxes
Wrapping paper in desired colors
    and patterns
Small pieces of ribbon in
    coordinating colors
Crafts glue; scissors; tape
Hot-glue gun and glue sticks
Small piece of cording
Purchased small bow

HERE'S HOW

Wrap the jewelry boxes in desired colors
and patterns of wrapping paper. Use
crafts glue to glue ribbons around the
wrapped boxes. Hot-glue the three boxes
together with the largest box on the
bottom. Hot glue the cording to the top
for hanging. Glue the small purchased
bow over the cording.

Felt Cutouts

Shown on page 14

WHAT YOU NEED

Tracing paper or copier
Pencil; scissors
Red, blue, yellow, and white felt scraps
Sharp pinking shears
Sharp paper punch
Fabric marking pen; fabric glue
Embroidery floss to match felt
Three 7-inch lengths thin metallic cord

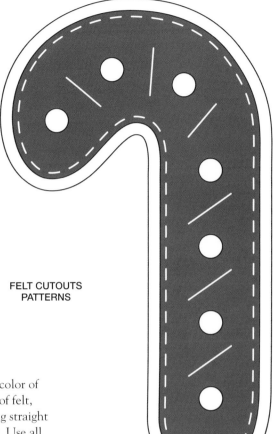

FELT CUTOUTS PATTERNS

HERE'S HOW

Trace or copy desired pattern, *above left* and *above*, and cut out. Decide which colors to use for top and middle layers of ornaments. Consider whether to cut with regular straight-edge scissors or pinking shears. With fabric marking pen, trace around pattern onto top felt piece, cutting two to make ornaments two-sided. Lay pattern onto center felt color and cut one piece slightly larger than the pattern piece. Using the same color of floss as the larger center piece of felt, stitch running stitches and long straight stitches on both smaller pieces. Use all six strands of embroidery floss. Fold cord in half to make hanging loop and glue to the top back of one smaller shape. Glue stitched pieces to both sides of the larger center piece.

Christmas Green Trims

Shown on page 15

WHAT YOU NEED

Purchased green matte-finish
   Christmas ornaments
Crafts glue; toothpick
Glitter
Small jewels
Glittery alphabet stickers

HERE'S HOW

1. To make the jeweled ball, place dots of glue on the ball in desired places. Use toothpick to pull out star shapes of glue from glue dots. Dust with glitter. Immediately add a jewel to the center of glitter and glue. Allow to dry. Repeat for other side.
2. To make the "joy" ball, adhere the alphabet stickers to the ball. Add a drop of glue for the dot of the J. Place jewel on the dot. Allow to dry.

Choose printed papers and trims that fit your holiday theme and create pretty paper projects that everyone will love!

playful
paper holiday

With just a little paper and some touches of glitter and ribbon you

can create **Folded Christmas Trees**, *opposite* and *above*. Start

with two-sided printed papers and then cut and fold the trees into

ornaments or clever cards. Instructions are on page 32.

This Christmas, add to your family's holiday traditions by making an Advent calendar. Customize the **Full of Treats Advent Calendar** by choosing favorite papers and accents. Glue the trims to a premade Advent box-style calendar. Your family will look forward to opening a drawer each day to reveal a tiny gift. Instructions are on page 33.

Cut in the shapes of traditional ornaments, these **Paper Pocket Ornaments**, *opposite*, are perfect for using leftover pieces of scrapbook paper. The paper is sewn together to form little pockets that hold Christmas goodies.

If you plan to make your own Christmas cards this year, consider **Joyful Greetings**, *left*. The designs are quick to make and send a simply perfect holiday message. Instructions are on pages 33–36.

This is a star.
At Christmas, we read about
the Star of Bethlehem.
We might see a star sparkling at
the top of a Christmas tree.

Can you find the stars?

Shapes are all around us,
every day of the year.
We can even find shapes in
some special things we see
only at Christmas.

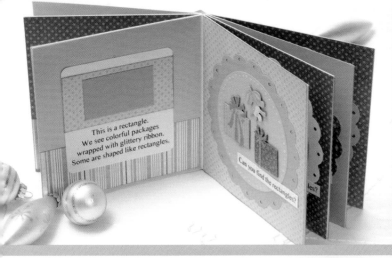

This is a rectangle.
We see colorful packages
wrapped with glittery ribbon.
Some are shaped like rectangles.

Can you find the rectangles?

Look around to see all the
fun shapes that Christmas
brings—then make a fun book
to read when you cuddle up
with your little one. This
**Little Christmas Shapes
Book** uses a ready-made
blank book, but you also can
recyle an old children's board
book for the base. Instructions
are on pages 36–37.

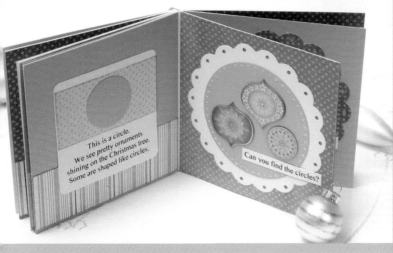

This is a circle.
We see pretty ornaments
shining on the Christmas tree.
Some are shaped like circles.

Can you find the circles?

This is a triangle.
A Christmas tree looks like a
triangle. A church steeple looks
like a triangle, too.

Can you find the triangles?

Look around you.
What special shapes can YOU
find this Christmas?

Quilling is a traditional and lovely paper art. Create **Delicate Quilled Ornaments,** *opposite,* using tiny purchased precut strips of paper or cut your own paper to the width you like. Shape the tiny spiraled strips into wreaths, candy canes, snowflakes, or other wintery motifs. Add trims of ribbon, bells, or jewels for more sparkle and dimension. Instructions and patterns are on page 37.

2. Make crisp accordion-pleat folds back and forth, folding back the smallest section first. If using as a package decoration or tree ornament, punch a small hole in the top point through all thicknesses using a sharp awl point. Thread a length of decorative cording through the hole and tie ends together. Smaller trees can be used for card decorations by simply gluing in place along long back edge of paper.

Folded Christmas Trees
Shown on page 22–23

WHAT YOU NEED
Tracing paper or copier
Pencil
Two-sided patterned cardstock
Awl
Thin decorative cording
Straight edge and pinking shears

HERE'S HOW
1. Trace patterns onto tracing paper or photocopy desired size pattern. Trace onto patterned cardstock. Cut half circle shape using either straight edge or pinking shears.

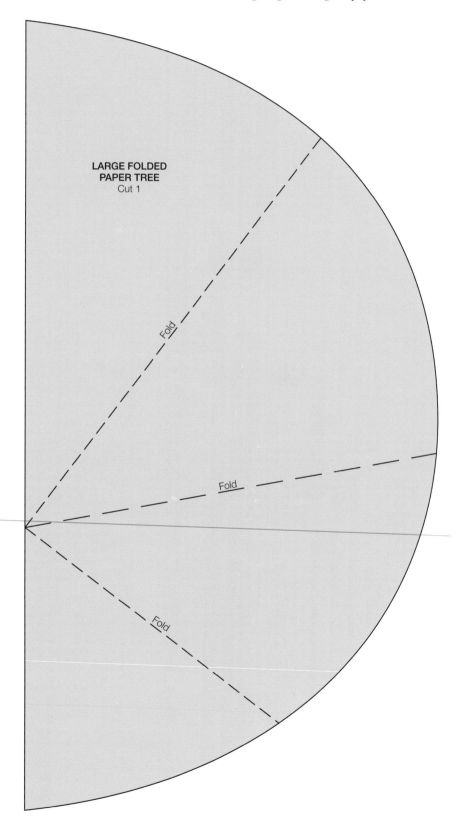

LARGE FOLDED
PAPER TREE
Cut 1

Fold

Fold

Fold

Full of Treats Advent Calendar

Shown on pages 24–25

WHAT YOU NEED

Purchased Countdown Calendar box,
    such as Karen Foster (includes
    calendar and number stickers)
Patterned paper
Cardstock
Stickers, large brads, and rub-ons
Diecut letters
Ink
Wire cutters; trimmer
Adhesive; glue dots
Circle punch
Scissors; ruler
Wave trimmer
Glitter glue
25 miniature toys or treats to fit drawers

HERE'S HOW

1. Select a coordinated line of paper for
this project. Choose paper with a variety
of small-scale patterns and colors.
As an alternative, decorate the Advent
calendar with leftover bits of paper
and embellishments.
2. Measure each drawer and cut 25
pieces of patterned paper to fit, mixing
patterns and colors as desired.
3. Punch a half-hole in the top edge
of each piece to match the notches on
the drawers.
4. Use stickers, rub-ons, and large brads
to decorate each piece, then ink the
edges and adhere to drawers. (Cut the
prongs from large brads using wire cutters;
adhere decorative brad top with glue dots.)
5. Cut paper to fit the sides and back
of advent calendar box; ink and adhere.
6. Decorate the top of the calendar if
desired: Cut a cardstock background
and reinforce with chipboard; adhere
to back side of calendar. Decorate with
stickers, die cuts, and glitter glue. Or
purchase Christmas figurines or wooden
letters, paint if necessary, and affix to the
top of the calendar with hot glue.

Paper Pocket Ornaments

Shown on page 26

WHAT YOU NEED

Tracing paper
Pencil; scissors
Assorted coordinating decorative
    papers
Glue stick
Heavy craft glue
Small pieces of ribbon, rickrack,
    and other trims
Fine metallic cording
Sewing machine; sewing thread

HERE'S HOW

1. Trace desired patterns on pages 34–35.
Cut ornament back pattern and
ornament front (pocket) pattern from
desired decorative papers. Cut ornament
top from gold metallic paper.

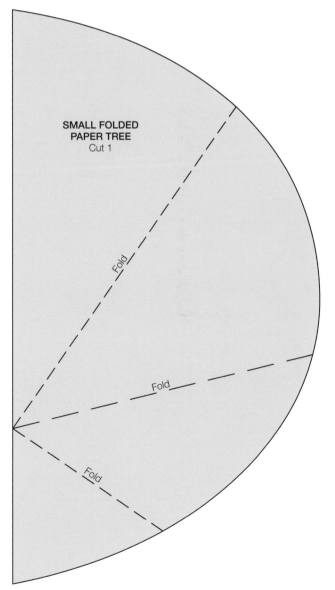

SMALL FOLDED
PAPER TREE
Cut 1

Fold

Fold

Fold

playful paper holiday

2. Using glue stick for paper and heavier craft glue for trims, embellish ornament back and pocket. Cut a 7-inch piece of cording, fold in half, and place at the top of ornament, gluing in place with a dot of craft glue. Place gold ornament top over cording and glue in place.

3. After trims dry, place pocket piece on top of ornament back and machine-stitch around outside and lower edges using sewing thread.

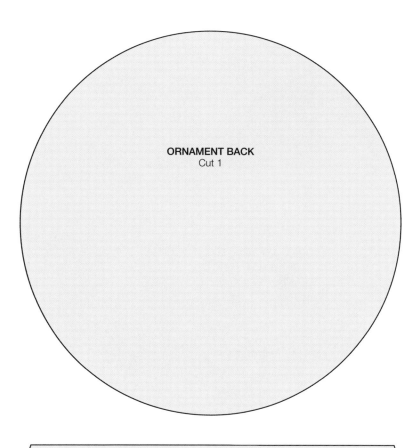

ORNAMENT BACK
Cut 1

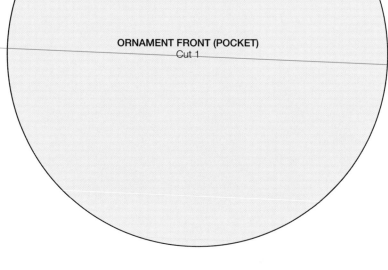

ORNAMENT FRONT (POCKET)
Cut 1

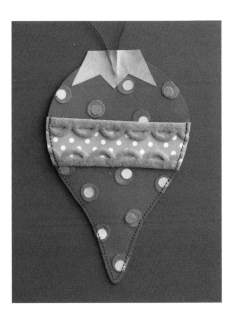 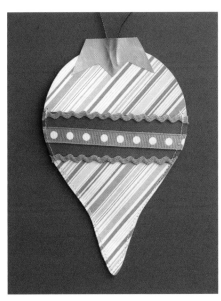

Joyful Greetings
Shown on page 27

WHAT YOU NEED FOR THE JOY CARD
Cardstock
Patterned paper and die-cut tree,
    such as My Mind's Eye
Die-cut letters, such as QuicKutz
Brads
Ink such as Fluid Chalk by Colorbox
Trimmer; ruler
Adhesive
Foam dots such as Pop Dots
Corner rounder
Paper piercer or awl
Circle cutter; scoring tool
Computer/printer for printing
    inside greeting

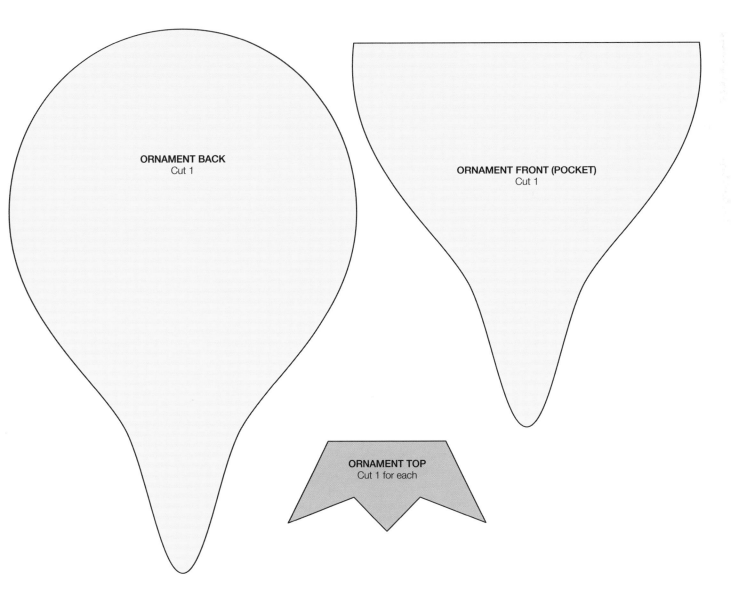

ORNAMENT BACK
Cut 1

ORNAMENT FRONT (POCKET)
Cut 1

ORNAMENT TOP
Cut 1 for each

Note: If you do not have die-cut Christmas trees to use on your cards, you can easily make your own, (see pattern, *below*). You also can substitute sticker letters for die-cut letters and stamp or write the inside greeting instead of printing it on a computer.

HERE'S HOW TO MAKE THE "JOY" CARD

1. Cut an 8½×11-inch sheet of cardstock in half lengthwise to create card base (4¼×11 inches). Score and fold in half so card opens at bottom. Round corners and ink the edges.

2. Cut a 4¼×2-inch strip of patterned paper. Ink and adhere across the bottom edge of the card.

3. Use a circle cutter to cut a 4-inch circle from contrasting cardstock. Cut in half (save the other half for another card). Ink the edges and adhere to the left side of the card.

4. Use a paper-piercing tool to make three small holes in the die-cut tree. Insert brads. Ink the edges of the tree and adhere to the front of the card using foam pop dots.

5. Adhere "JOY" to the front of the card.

6. Print or stamp an inside greeting for the card.

WHAT YOU NEED FOR THE "BE JOLLY" CARD

Cardstock
Patterned paper and die-cut snowman such as My Mind's Eye
Die-cut letters such as QuickKutz
Buttons
Ink such as Fluid Chalk by Colorbox
Trimmer
Adhesive
Foam dots such as Pop Dots
Corner rounder
Paper piercer
Circle cutter
Scoring tool
Computer/printer for printing inside greeting

Note: If you do not have die-cut snowmen to use on your cards, you can easily make your own, (see pattern, *below*). You also can substitute sticker letters for die-cut letters and stamp or write your inside greeting instead of printing it on a computer.

HERE'S HOW TO MAKE THE "BE JOLLY" CARD

1. Cut an 8½-inch sheet of cardstock in half width wise to create card base (5½×8½ inches). Score and fold in half so that card opens at bottom.

2. Round corners and ink the edges.

3. Cut two 1½×1½-inch squares from contrasting cardstock and ink the edges.

Cut a 2¼×3¼-inch rectangle from a third color of cardstock and ink the edges. Adhere all three pieces to the front of the card.

4. Adhere die-cut snowman using foam dots.

5. Adhere "Be Jolly" text to the top square.

6. Adhere three buttons to the bottom square using glue dots.

7. Print or stamp an inside greeting for your card.

Little Christmas Shapes Book

Shown on pages 28–29

WHAT YOU NEED

6×6-inch board book, such as Bo Bunny
Patterned paper, such as Imaginesce by Bo Bunny
Cardstock
Chipboard die cuts, such as K&Company
Glitter alphabets, such as Making Memories
Ribbon

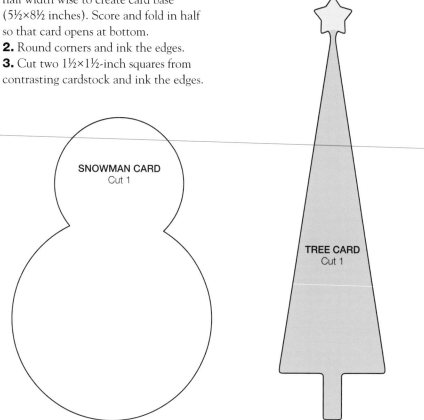

SNOWMAN CARD
Cut 1

TREE CARD
Cut 1

Glitter glue, such as Stickles by Ranger
Ink, such as Fluid Chalk by Colorbox
Trimmer; adhesive
Foam dots, such as Pop Dots
Corner rounder
Circle punch; small hole punch
Circle cutter; scissors
Computer and printer
Star punch; die-cutting machine
Scalloped circle die cuts, such as
   AccuCut

HERE'S HOW

1. Determine the theme for your project and select appropriate products. Because this is a book about shapes, the chipboard die cuts are chosen because they include simple images of the desired shapes. Select paper and cardstock to match the selected products.
2. Plan a simple design. To achieve a cohesive look, repeat the same designs throughout the book. For instance, in this book scalloped circles and patterned paper strips are repeated on each page.
3. Trim cardstock and patterned paper to fit the cover and inside pages of the book. Ink the edges as desired and adhere to the book base.
4. Write the text for your book and format it on the computer.
5. Print and adhere text to each page.
6. Ink the scalloped circles and cut contrasting circles for the centers. Add glitter glue and allow to dry. Adhere to pages of book.

7. Adhere die-cut chipboard to "illustrate" your story. Be sure to use strong adhesive.
8. Decorate the cover with ribbon, glitter alphabet letters, and a chipboard shape.

Delicate Quilled Ornaments
Shown on pages 30–31

WHAT YOU NEED
⅛-inch-wide white, green, and
   red paper quilling strips at least
   12 inches long, or paper cut
   to fit dimensions
White glue
Toothpicks
Plastic circle template
Scissors
Hanging thread
Assorted sizes of round
   acrylic gemstones
Assorted ribbons
Buttons
Assorted sequins
⅜-inch jingle bells
Glue

HERE'S HOW

Following diagrams, *right*, and instructions, *below*, cut lengths for paper strips and circle sizes. Assemble pieces, attach hanger cords and accents.
For the candy cane, spiral and glue together 6-inch-long red and white quills. Use ⅜-inch ribbon, tie once, trim, and glue on as accent.
For the wreath, make quills from 6-inch paper, spiral, and glue together. Use a ⅜-inch ribbon and two small jingle bells as accents.
For the snowflake, fold two 6-inch-long quills in half and roll up each end. Glue one spiral inside the other. Entire snowflake frame is made of 6 spirals glued together at the base. Five large center spirals are 6-inch-long quills spiraled and glued in place. Glue gem accents at the center front and back as desired.

**DELICATE
QUILLED
ORNAMENTS**
Full-Size
Diagrams

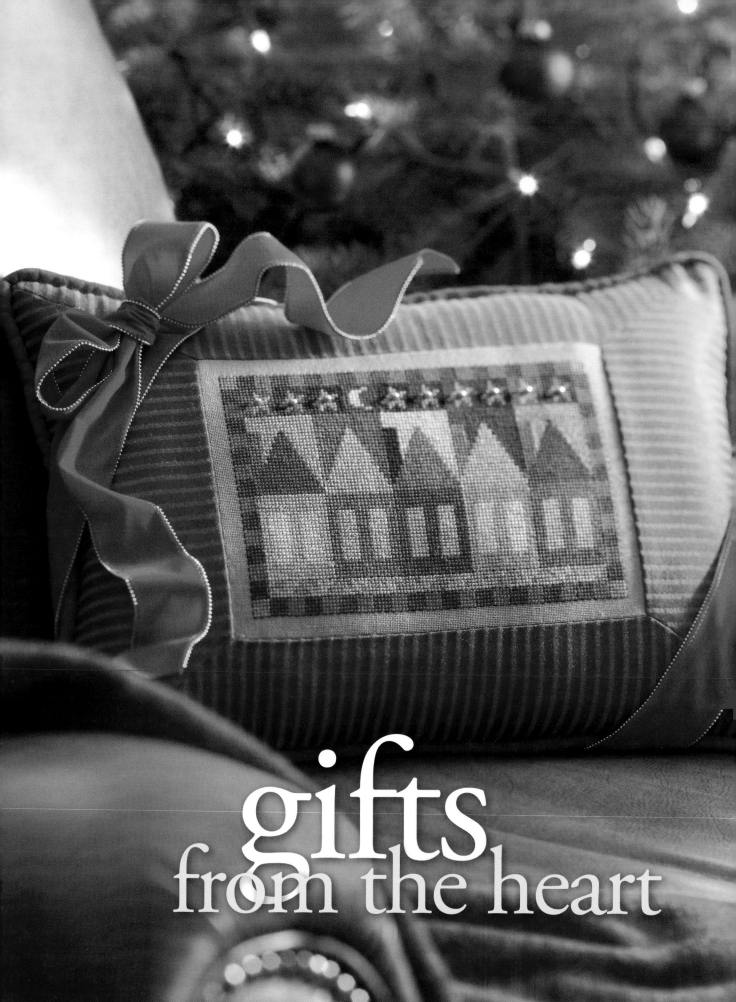

gifts
from the heart

Whether you like to quilt, knit, paint, cross-stitch, sew, bead, or just assemble wonderful personalized gifts—you will find the perfect present for everyone on your holiday gift list.

Sure to become a treasured gift, **Christmas Neighborhood Cross-Stitch**, *opposite*, can be worked up in time for Christmas. Make it into a pillow for holiday decorating or finish it as a framed piece of art. Let the whole family help add a personal touch to every gift by making **Color Me Gift Tags**, *above*. Simply copy the tags and color them to coordinate with holiday wrapping. Instructions are on page 48.

CHOCOLATE
CHUNK
PECAN
MUFFINS

Breakfast
Cornbread

Maple
Syrup

Simple canning jars are a
favorite way to present
food gifts. This year offer
Breakfast Goodie Jars
filled with ingredients to
make a quick and healthy
Christmas morning
breakfast. Instructions for
the jars are on page 50. The
recipes are on page 160.

Breakfast
Oatmeal
Mix

Going green is easy when you stitch **Carry-Along Bags.** Make these clever bags in any color you choose and paint a quick design on the pocket-style carrier. Instructions are on page 50.

She'll love a **Wool Poinsettia Pin**, *right,* to wear on her coat at Christmastime. The beads in the center make the blossom appear almost real. So sweet yet so practical, a **Tiny Felted Purse**, *bottom right,* is a perfect party clutch. Add a few embroidery stitches and give to a favorite friend. Bring back playful gum-wrapper art using pretty wrapping paper to make **Folded Paper Play**, *opposite,* that can be used for so many gifts. Create frames or ornaments with this easy folding technique. Instructions and patterns are on pages 51-53.

Scraps of fabric and leftover jewels combine to make **Yo-Yo Flower Pins,** *above left,* that dress up any holiday outfit. **Practical Pot Holders,** *above right,* use felted wool scraps sewn together with a buttonhole stitch. Create Clever **Beaded Bookmarks,** *right,* for the avid reader on your Christmas list. Instructions are on pages 54–55.

Sparkling beads in red and green become Christmas tree jewelry. Create **Tree Earrings** or **Tree Bauble** using a single beaded tree. Add the bauble to a **Holiday Bracelet** or make a larger version for a **Christmas Tree Zipper Pull**. Instructions are on pages 55–56.

Knit a **Cabled Scarf and Bag,**
above, for someone special on
your Christmas list. Give a card
and a gift all in one with a
Snowman Pin Greeting Card,
right. Use scraps of wool and
pretty buttons for the snowman
and add a stamped greeting.
Instructions are on pages 56–57.

Christmas
Wishes

Teach that sweet little one some new tricks with a stitched **Busy Baby Book** that shares all kinds of fun activities. Buttoning, tying, matching, counting, and touching make this busy book a favorite. Instructions and patterns are on pages 57–61.

Christmas Neighborhood Cross-Stitch

Shown on page 38

WHAT YOU NEED

6½×9½-inch piece of tan Aida cloth
Cotton embroidery floss in colors listed
   in key on page 49
Cross-stitch needle; embroidery hoop
Scissors; iron
9 gold 4-mm beads
½ yard red striped upholstery fabric
⅛ yard red suede-like fabric
1⅔ yards of ⅜-wide cording
Matching sewing thread
12×16-inch pillow form
2¼ yards of 1½-inch-wide decorative
   wire-edge ribbon

HERE'S HOW

1. Find the center of the chart and the center of the fabric; begin stitching there. Use two plies of floss for all cross-stitches. Work the backstitches using one ply of floss. Press piece on back side. Sew gold bead onto center of each star at the top of pattern.
2. To make the pillow, overcast piece edges to prevent raveling. For overlapping pillow back, cut striped fabric into two 11¼×12½-inch pieces. For pillow front, cut striped fabric into two 4½×15-inch lengths and two 3¾×20-inch lengths. To cover cording with red fabric, cut strips 1¾×60 inches. Sew 4½-inch pieces of striped fabric to side edges of stitchery using ¼-inch seam allowances, starting and stopping stitching at seam line corners of stitchery. Sew longer edges of 3¾-inch pieces to top and bottom of stitchery, also starting and stopping at corners. Miter corners of strips by

folding back pieces to meet at outside corners. Use fold lines to stitch mitered seams; press.
3. For pillow backing, fold under ¼ inch along raw edge of both 12½-inch sides. Fold under another inch and press flat. Sew sections along fold edges to hem in place. Overlap sections 3 inches and baste across edges. Cover cording with red fabric. Sew cording to pillow top, clipping at corners. With right sides together sew pillow front to back around all sides, using ⅜-inch seam. Using back slit turn pillow right side out. Insert pillow form.
4. Cut one length of ribbon 44 inches long to wrap around corners of pillow, starting and ending at the back. With remaining length of ribbon, tie a bow and tack onto one corner of ribbon.

Color Me Gift Tags

Shown on page 39

WHAT YOU NEED

Copier
Fine tip markers or colored pencils
White cardstock
Scissors
Double-sided clear tape or glue dots
Small hole paper punch
Metallic thread

HERE'S HOW

1. Copy desired design onto cardstock and print.
2. Color tags as desired. Use dots of color on evergreen or pine boughs.
3. Cut out tags. Attach to packages with double-sided clear tape or glue dots. Or punch a tiny hole in tag and attach a thread to tie to a bow on a package.

COLOR ME GIFT TAGS
Full-Size Patterns

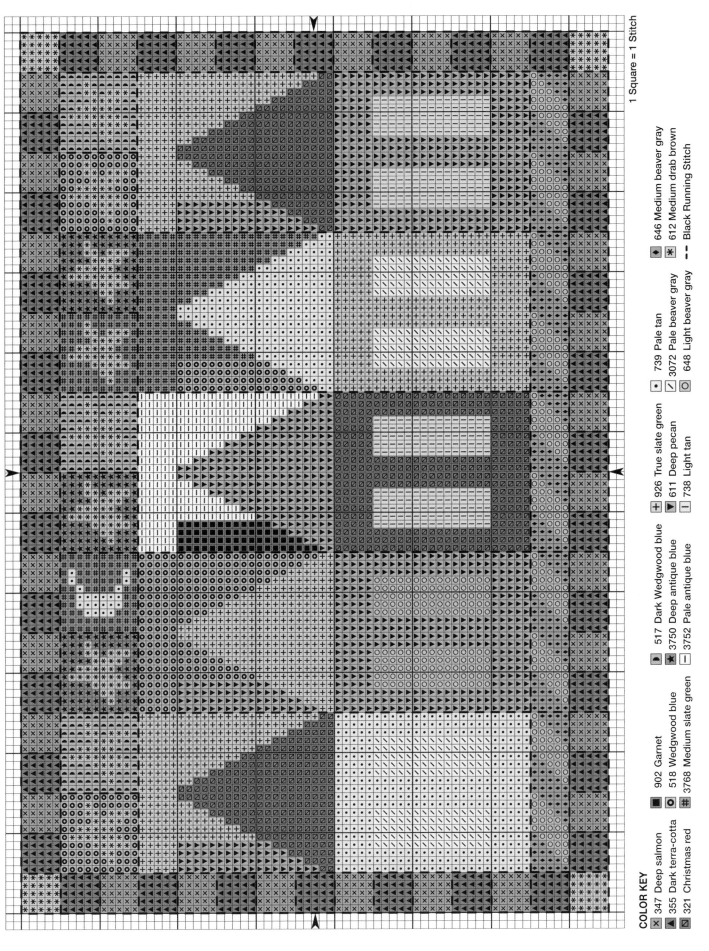

1 Square = 1 Stitch

COLOR KEY

☒	347 Deep salmon	▣	517 Dark Wedgwood blue	•	739 Pale tan	◆ 646 Medium beaver gray
◀	355 Dark terra-cotta	★	3750 Deep antique blue	⧄	3072 Pale beaver gray	✳ 612 Medium drab brown
☑	321 Christmas red	⊟	3752 Pale antique blue	◯	648 Light beaver gray	⎯ Black Running Stitch
■	902 Garnet	⊞	926 True slate green			
◯	518 Wedgwood blue	▶	611 Deep pecan			
#	3768 Medium slate green	⊺	738 Light tan			

Breakfast Goodie Jars
Shown on page 40

WHAT YOU NEED
Quart canning jars
Scrapbook paper in desired colors
Scissors; pencil
Ingredients and tag for recipe chosen
   (See page 160 for recipes)
Narrow ribbon

HERE'S HOW
Be sure the jar is clean and dry. Trace around the jar lid onto desired scrapbook paper. Cut out. Make tag that tells additional ingredients to add to the dry ingredients, method, and directions on how to finish preparation. Set aside. Prepare dry ingredients for desired recipe. Carefully put dry ingredients into jar. Assemble lid, paper, and screw top on jar. Add rickrack, ribbons, or other desired tie on. Add label.

Carry-Along Bags
Shown on page 41

WHAT YOU NEED
Tracing paper
Pencil; scissors
¾ yard nylon
   ripstop fabric
Matching sewing thread
1-inch piece of Velcro
Small piece of cardboard
Fabric paint in desired color
Paintbrush

HERE'S HOW
1. Trace or copy the case pattern, *below*. Set aside. Cut one piece 18×36 inches to use as the main body of the bag. Cut two 27×2¼-inch strips for handles. Cut two from the case pattern. Cut one 8½×8½-inch square for pocket.
2. Prepare pocket by stitching ¼ inch around side and lower edges. This will provide a guide for turning under edges when stitching to bag body because the ripstop fabric does not iron well. Fold top edge of pocket ¼ inch to back side and then another 1 inch. Stitch close to folds to hem top. Fold in side and lower edges just past the ¼-inch stitching line while

pinning the pocket in place about 7¼ inches from top center of bag body. Stitch close to folded edges around side and lower edges of pocket, reinforcing at top edges while sewing pocket to bag.
3. With right sides together, fold bag main body in half to make an 18-inch square. Sew side seams of bag. At bottom corners at side seam, flatten bag right sides together with the side seam matching the bottom fold of the bag to make a triangle at corners to allow for depth in the bag bottom. Sew across the end about 1½ inches from the point. Turn bag right side out.
Note: Fabric ravels easily so consider sewing with a French seam, overcast the edges, or use a serger to sew the seams.
4. With right sides together fold handles in half lengthwise. Stitch long edges together in a ¼-inch seam. Turn right side out and stitch close to both side edges. Turn top edge of bag ¼ inch to inside and again another 1 inch. Pin in place. Place handles 5 inches from the sides of the bag and pin in place so one handle is looped over each side of the bag top, tucking handle raw edge just under lower edge of the bag's top hem. Sew close to both folded edges of bag top hem, backstitching at handles to reinforce.
5. For case, place two case pieces right sides together and sew both top angled

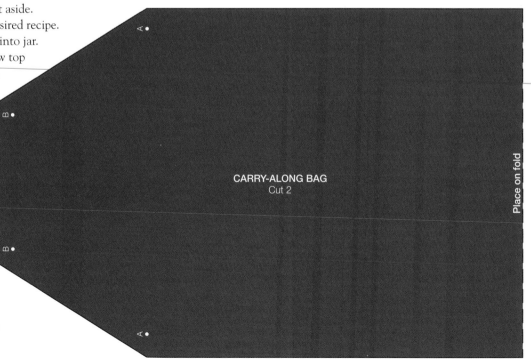

CARRY-ALONG BAG
Cut 2

Place on fold

edges together in a ¼-inch seam, stitching from point A to point B, as marked on the pattern. Turn right side out and sew close to folded edges. Place right sides together and sew side edges in a ¼-inch seam. On inside, flatten bottom corners together at side seam and sew a small triangle across bottom about ½-inch from point of side seam. This gives depth to the case. Sew small pieces of Velcro to top openings, stitching close to outside edges of Velcro.

6. Place cardboard inside case and use fabric paint and paintbrush to decorate case desired.

7. To insert bag into case, fold bag lengthwise in half and then in thirds, tuck in handles, then fold crosswise and roll up remaining length to slide easily into case.

Wool Poinsettia Pin
Shown on page 42

WHAT YOU NEED
Tracing paper or copier; pencil
Scraps red and green
    felted wool (see page 160
    for felting instructions)
Needle
Red and green metallic
    embroidery floss
Matching sewing thread
7 gold glass seed beads
1½-inch pin back

HERE'S HOW
1. Trace or copy patterns, *below*. Cut one center leaf pattern from red felted wool and one middle leaf pattern from red felted wool. Cut one green leaf pattern from green felted wool.

2. See stitch diagrams on page 160. Using one strand of red metallic embroidery floss, sew center leaf vein lines using a stem outline stitch on center of red wool piece. If you pull the decorative stitches fairly tightly, the wool piece curls slightly. Sew vein lines on middle red wool piece in the same manner. Using one strand of green metallic embroidery floss, sew vein lines on green leaf piece of wool.

3. Layer three pieces of wool, staggering leaves. Using red sewing thread, make a couple of stitches in the center to anchor all pieces together. Sew seven gold glass beads in center of top wool piece. Sew pin back across back of green wool piece.

Tiny Felted Purse
Shown on page 42

WHAT YOU NEED
Tracing paper and marking pen
2×9-inch scraps of felted
    red wool (see page 160
    for felting instructions)
Scissors
1-inch strip of Velcro
Matching sewing thread; needle
Green embroidery floss
Metallic red and green embroidery floss
Three ½-inch red buttons
½ yard narrow braided red trim

**WOOL POINSETTIA PIN
LAYER 3
Cut 1**

**WOOL POINSETTIA PIN
LAYER 2
Cut 1**

**WOOL POINSETTIA PIN
LAYER 1
Cut 1**

HERE'S HOW

1. Trace or copy pattern, *right*. Set aside. Felt wool fabric by washing in hot water and drying fabric in a hot dryer. Press. Cut two purse pieces from felted wool. Sew Velcro strips to rounded edge of lining piece and the other Velcro strip to the short straight end of the outside piece of wool.

2. With right sides together stitch across bottom straight edge of purse, using a ¼-inch seam. Mark placement of holly on outside rounded edge of purse. Using two strands of green floss, sew stem outline stitch around leaves and center lines of leaves. Using one strand green metallic floss, stitch another stem outline stitch close to center leaf line. Using red metallic embroidery thread, sew tiny red buttons at center of leaves.

3. With right sides together measure up 6½ inches from bottom straight edge of purse and mark with pins at both side edges. Using a ¼-inch seam sew from pin around the top curve to the other pin at the side edge. Remove pins. Turn right side out and press edges flat. Sew red trim around top curved edge, tacking on by hand with matching sewing thread. Using one strand red metallic embroidery floss, make decorative lazy daisy stitches around curved edge onto wool. With right sides together fold bottom straight edge up about 3 inches and sew side seams in ¼-inch seams. Turn right side out and press side seams flat. Measure 7½ inches of trim for handle and attach at back side edges just under the folded flap.

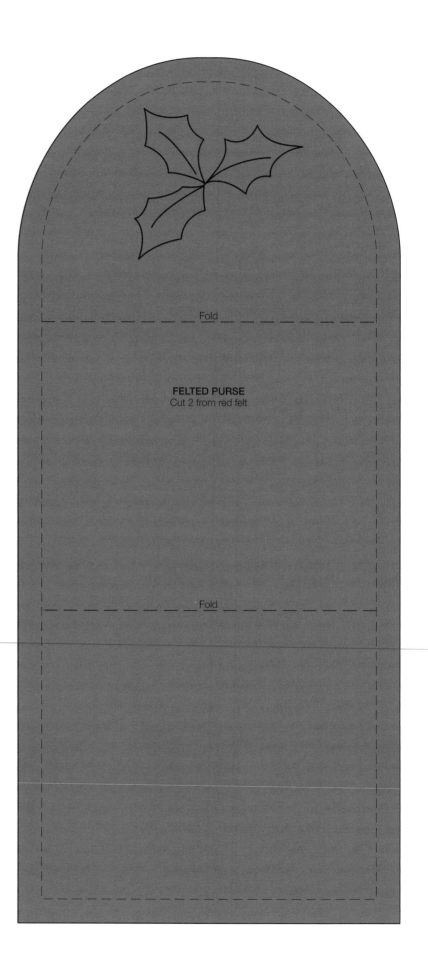

Fold

FELTED PURSE
Cut 2 from red felt

Fold

Folded Paper Play

Shown on page 43

WHAT YOU NEED FOR THE PICTURE FRAME

Acrylic picture frame or frame with flat
faces narrow enough to be covered
Lightweight scrapbook papers
Hot-glue gun; glue sticks; toothpicks
Scissors or paper cutter
Tracing paper; pencil
Sequins or acrylic gemstones
Metallic ribbon

HERE'S HOW TO MAKE THE PICTURE FRAME

1. Cut and fold paper according to the
diagrams, *right*. Connect pieces forming
four straight strips to fit size of frame
chosen. Use the frame as a guide for
lengths. Corners should form a square
or a squared-off corner. Allow for right
angles so frame corner will be covered
when assembled. Join one corner by
placing a small dot of hot glue on inside
of paper chain. Attach adjoining chain
forming squared off corner. Continue for
all four corners. Glue paper chain to
frame by running a thin bead of glue
along back of chain; place on frame.
2. Trace and cut out holly patterns from
green scrapbook paper. To make holly
appear more real, run the tip of a toothpick
over vein lines while holding paper taut
against table. Pull to lift paper to the sides
of the toothpick. Then attach to frame
corner with a dab of hot glue on a toothpick.
Add sequins or acrylic gemstones for the
holly berries and ribbon for accent.

WHAT YOU NEED FOR THE CANDY CANE

Foil paper Christmas gift wraps in
2–3 coordinating papers
Scissors or paper cutter
Hot-glue gun; glue sticks
Sequins or acrylic gemstones
Toothpicks; ribbons
Holly cutouts, jingle bells; other
desired trims

HERE'S HOW TO MAKE THE CANDY CANE

1. Cut and fold paper according to the
diagrams, *right*.
2. Alternate papers as desired or use a
one-color paper scheme. Connect enough
pieces (refer to photo, *above* and page 43)
for candy canes. While folding, gently
coax the folded paper chain into
a curve. The pieces will slide a little
to accommodate the curve if it is not
too severe. **Note:** Use a toothpick with
a tiny dab of hot glue for foil paper.
It sets immediately and adheres better
to the foil surface.
3. Add ribbon bow, sequins for holly
berries, cutout holly leaves, small buttons,
hanging thread or other trims as desired.

FOLDED PAPER PLAY
Holly Pattern

WHAT YOU NEED FOR THE WREATH ORNAMENT

Scrapbook or wrapping papers in
coordinating prints or other selected
papers
White glue
Toothpick
Scissors or paper cutter
Hanging thread
Tiny buttons or jingle bells
Sequins or acrylic gemstones
Ribbon
Holly cutouts or other desired trims

FOLDED PAPER PLAY
Folding Diagrams

Diagram 1

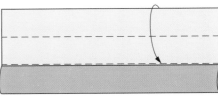

Diagram 2

Diagram 3

Diagram 4

Diagram 5

Diagram 6

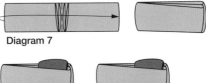

Diagram 7

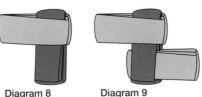

Diagram 8   Diagram 9

HERE'S HOW TO MAKE THE WREATH ORNAMENT

1. Cut and fold paper according to the diagrams, page 53.

2. Alternate papers as desired or use a one-color paper scheme. Connect enough pieces (refer to photo, *above* and page 43) for wreath. As you work gently coax the folded paper chain into a curve. The pieces will slide a little to accommodate the curve if it is not too severe.

3. Add ribbon bow, sequins for holly berries, cutout holly leaves, small buttons, hanging thread, or other trims as desired. **Note**: To make cutting quicker, cut paper in multiples of the length needed; fold and then cut individual pieces from the folded length.

Yo-Yo Flower Pins
Shown on page 44

WHAT YOU NEED
Tracing paper
Fabric scraps (12-inch diameter for large, 10-inch diameter for medium, 7-inch diameter for small)
Matching sewing thread; needle
Decorative buttons, brooches, discarded earrings
1½-inch pin backs
Crafts glue

HERE'S HOW
Make a circle pattern in desired size on the tracing paper and cut out. We used a 12-inch circle for the large, 10-inch for medium, and 7-inch for small yo-yos.

Cut fabric from desired size circle pattern. Make yo-yo by turning under outside edge a scant ¼-inch and sewing a long running stitch around outside edge. Using a double thread helps to avoid breaking the thread as the stitching is pulled up

tightly to the center. Take a couple of stabilizing stitches in the center of the yo-yo to secure the gathering. Pull the needle up through the center, then around the outside edge of the yo-yo, going over the outside fold to the center back. Pull the thread tight while drawing the needle through the center back to the front. Make five of these over the edge stitches around the circle to make five petals. Sew on a decorative button, pin brooch, or glue other jewelry to front. Sew pin to back side.

Practical Pot Holders
Shown on page 44

WHAT YOU NEED
Discarded wool sweaters
Scissors; ruler
Straight pins
Scraps cotton batting
Yarn; darning needle
Crochet hook

HERE'S HOW

1. Felt wool sweaters. **Note:** For felting instructions, see page 160. Cut two 7-inch squares from felted wool sweaters for each pot holder. Cut one 6½-inch square from cotton batting.

2. Add decorative stitches to top side of wool squares, as desired, using contrasting yarn. Pot holders shown use lazy daisy stitch for flowers, French knots for centers, stem outline stitch for swirls, and running stitch.

3. Sandwich batting between layers of wool and pin together around edges. Use yarn and large darning needle to sew a whipstitch or blanket stitch around the edges through both layers of wool, beginning and ending at one corner. At corner, continue the length of yarn in a single crochet chain to make a loop, connecting at the beginning stitching.

Beaded Bookmarks
Shown on page 44

WHAT YOU NEED

20 inches of 1.0-mm stretchy
    beading cord
5 crimp beads
Assortment of beads to make 7 inches
Assortment of beads and charms
    for tassel
Scissors
Crimping tool

HERE'S HOW

1. Fold cord in half to find center. Attach crimp bead approximately 1 inch to one side of the center of the cord. Arrange, then string approximately 7 inches of beads on the shorter side of the cord. Attach a crimp bead at the bottom of the beads, leaving about 2 inches of cord for the tassel.

2. String both ends of cord through the last bead, aligning the ends of the cord. String both ends of cord through one crimp bead and crimp close to the last bead.

3. String beads and charms for the tassel on each of the two ends of cord. Attach crimp bead below tassel beads. **Note:** This bookmark will fit a standard size paperback book or smaller size hardcover book. For a larger book, use longer cord and more beads.

Holiday Bracelet
Shown on page 45

WHAT YOU NEED

10 to 12 inches of .48-mm diameter
    clear-coated flexible stainless steel
    beading wire
1 silver 6-mm split ring
1 silver 10-mm lobster-claw clasp
2 silver crimp beads
16 green 4×8-mm disc beads
8 red 10-mm round beads
7 silver 4-mm round beads
Wire cutters
Crimping tool

HERE'S HOW

Attach clasp to one end of wire and crimp tightly. String beads in order: green, red, green, silver, green. Hide short end of wire by stringing back through several beads. Repeat pattern until desired size is reached. String on crimp bead and split ring. String back through crimp bead and several adjacent beads. Crimp tightly and cut wire close to bead. Attach Tree Bauble (see page 56) to the split ring.

Christmas Tree Zipper Pull
Shown on page 45

WHAT YOU NEED

2 size 8/0 brown seed beads
2 green 5×10-mm disc beads
2 green 4×8-mm disc beads
1 green 3×6-mm disc bead
1 green 4-mm bicone bead
1 gold 3-mm round bead
One 2½-inch silver headpin
1 silver 20-mm lobster-claw clasp
1 silver 6-mm split ring
Round-nose pliers
Wire cutters

HERE'S HOW

Assemble beads on the headpin in the order listed. Using the round-nose pliers make a wrapped loop above the last bead. Attach the tree shape to the lobster-claw clasp with the split ring.

Tree Earrings or Tree Bauble

Shown on page 45

WHAT YOU NEED (FOR ONE TREE)

2 size 1 8/0 brown beads
1 green 4×8-mm disc bead
1 green 3×6-mm disc bead
1 green 4-mm bicone bead
1 gold 2.5-mm bead
1 silver 2-inch headpin
Round-nose pliers
Split ring (bauble); ear wires (earrings)

HERE'S HOW

Assemble beads on headpin in the order listed. Using the round-nose pliers, make a wrapped loop above the round gold bead. For Tree Earrings, attach to ear wire with the wrapped loop. For the Tree Bauble, attach to split ring on bracelet.

Cabled Scarf and Bag

Shown on page 46

Skill Level: Intermediate

Sizes: Scarf: 7×52 inches;
Bag: 6×8 inches

WHAT YOU NEED

Patons Classic Merino Wool, 100% wool, worsted weight yarn (223 yards per ball): Russet (206): Scarf 3 balls, bag 4 balls
Size 10 (6 mm) knitting needles or size needed to obtain gauge
Size 9 (5.5 mm) knitting needles
Cable needle (cn); yarn needle

Gauge:

16 sts and 20 rows = 4/10cm in St st with 2 strands of yarn and larger needles.
TAKE TIME TO CHECK GAUGE.

Special Abbreviations:

C4F: Slip next 2 sts onto a cn and leave at front of work, k2, then k2 from cn.
C7F: Slip next 3 sts onto a cn and leave at front of work. (K3, pl), then k3 from cn.
C7B: Slip next 4 sts onto a cn and leave at back of work. K3, then (pl, k3) from cn.
Sl 1: Slip next st purlwise and with yarn on WS.

Stitches Used:

Panel A
(worked over 17 sts; a rep of 28 rows).
Row 1 (RS): P1, (k3, p1) 4 times.
Row 2 and all WS rows: K1, (p3, k1) 4 times.
Rows 3 and 5: As Row 1.
Row 7: Pl, k3, pl, C7F, p1, k3, p1.
Rows 9 and 11: As Row 1.
Row 13: As Row 7.
Rows 15, 17, and 19: As Row 1.
Row 21: P1, C7B, C7F, p1.
Rows 23 and 25: As Row 1.
Row 27: As Row 21.
Row 28: As Row 2.
Rep Rows 1-28 for Panel A.

Panel B
(worked over 6 sts; a rep of 8 rows).
Row 1 (RS): P1, k4, p1.
Row 2 and all WS rows: K1, p4, k1.
Row 3: P1, C4F, p1.
Rows 5 and 7: As Row 1.
Row 8: As Row 2.
Rep Rows 1-8 for Panel B.

Note: Bag is worked from side to side.

SCARF

With 2 strands of yarn and larger needles, cast on 31 sts.
Row 1 (RS): K1, p1) 3 times, k1, work Row of Panel A, (k1, p1) 3 times, k1.
Row 2: (P1, k1) 3 times, p1, work Row 2 of Panel A, (p1, k1) 3 times, p1.
Row 3: (P1, k1) 3 times, p1, work Row 3 of Panel A, (p1, k1) 3 times, p1.
Row 4: (K1, p1) 3 times, k1, work Row 4 of Panel A, (k1, p1) 3 times, k1. Panel Pat is now in position. Rows 1-4 form Irish Moss pat. Cont in pat, keeping cont of Panel Pat A and Irish Moss pat until work from beg measures approx 50", ending with a WS row; bind off.

BAG

With 2 strands of yarn and smaller needles, cast on 31 sts.
Row 1: (RS): K1, work Row 1 of Panel A, [(k1, p1) 6 times, k1 for Irish Moss].
Row 2: [P1, (k1, p1) 6 times for Irish Moss], work Row 2 of Panel A, p1.
Row 3: K1, work Row 3 of Panel A, [(pl, k1) 6 times, p1 for Irish Moss].
Row 4: [K1, (p1, k1) 6 times for Irish Moss], work Row 4 of Panel A, p1. Panel A is now in position. Rows 1-4 form Irish Moss pat. Cont in pat, keeping cont of Panel A and Irish Moss pat until work from beg measures approx 2", ending with a WS row. Form eyelets for the tie as follows.
**Next Row: Pat 21 sts, yo, work k2tog, pat to end of row. Place marker at end of row. Work 3 rows even in pat.
Next Row: Pat 21 sts, yo, work k2tog, pat to end of row. Work even in pat until work from marked row measures approx 4", ending with a WS row**. Rep from ** to ** twice more, ending with a WS row.
Next Row: Pat 21 sts, yo, work k2tog, pat to end of row. Place marker at end of row. Work 3 rows even in pat.
Next Row: Pat 21 sts, yo, work k2tog, pat to end of row. Work even in pat until work from marked row measures approx 2", ending with a WS row. Bind off.
Bottom: With RS of work facing, pick up and k65 sts along bottom of bag. Beg with a p row, work 3 rows even in St st. Place marker at end of last row. Shape bottom,
Row 1: K1, * k6, k2tog, rep from * to end of row-57 sts.
Row 2 and alt rows: Purl.
Row 3: K1; * k5, k2tog, rep from * to end of row-49 sts.
Cont in same manner, dec 8 sts on every RS row until 17 sts rem. Break yarn, leaving a long end. Thread yarn into yarn

needle and through rem sts; tighten securely. Sew bottom and side seam. With WS of work facing, sew marked row and pick up row tog to create a ridge on RS.

Handle: With 2 strands of yarn and smaller needles, CO 5 sts.
Row 1: (K1, p1) twice, k1.
Row 2: (P1, k1) twice, p1.
Row 3: As Row 2.
Row 4: As Row 1.
Rep last 4 rows until Handle measures approx 42", ending with a WS row. Bind off. Sew Handle inside of Bag 1" from top edge.

Twisted Cord: Cut 6 strands of yarn 78" long. With both strands tog, hold one end and with someone holding other end, twist strands to the right until they begin to curl. Fold the 2 ends tog and tie in a knot so they will not unravel. The strands will now twist themselves tog. Adjust length if desired. Thread cord through the eyelet holes.

Tassel (make 2): Wind yarn around a plastic card 20 times. Break yarn, leaving a long end, and thread end through a needle. Slip needle through all loops and tie tightly. Remove card and wind another strand of yarn tightly around loops 5¾" below fold. Fasten securely. Cut through rem loops and trim ends evenly. Sew tassels to ends of cord.

Snowman Pin Greeting Card
Shown on page 46

WHAT YOU NEED
Felt scraps
Embroidery floss: orange, brown, black, and tan
One ⅜-inch button
Two ⅝-inch buttons
One 1½-inch pin back
Black paint pen
Cardstock; scissors; pinking shears
Stamp and ink pad; fine glitter

HERE'S HOW
To make the pin: Cut inside felt piece 1½×2¼ inches using straight-edge scissors. Cut outside felt piece 2×2¾ inches, using pinking shears.

Sew buttons onto the smaller felt piece. If the small button has four holes, leave the top two unsewn for the eyes. Use orange embroidery floss to sew smaller button to appear as carrot nose. If the small button does not have four holes, make small dots above the orange thread with a black paint pen for the eyes. Using black embroidery thread sew larger buttons below the small button for the snowman body sections. Using all six strands of brown embroidery floss, stitch stick arms beside the middle button, using a stem outline stitch or long straight stitches. Using all six strands of tan embroidery floss, take a small stitch just under the small button and tie a loose knot for the scarf. Tie knots in the ends of both lengths of thread for the scarf ends. Sew center felt piece onto the larger felt backing piece, using six strands of black embroidery floss and securing with a decorative buttonhole stitch. On back side stitch pin back in place, centering pin vertically.

To make the card: Cut cardstock paper 7×10 inches. Fold in half to make card 7×5 inches. On front of card cut an opening 3×2¼ inches starting 3 inches up from the bottom of the card. Stamp a greeting onto the card or write the message with marker. Run a line of glue around the cut opening and dust with glitter. Pin the snowman to the inside of the card under the front opening.

Busy Baby Book
Shown on page 47

General things to consider: When sewing on buttons, snaps, beads, and other embellishments use heavy thread, such as button thread, securing with several tight stitches to hold in place. Use fabrics that can be washed or wiped off so the book can be easily cleaned. Be sure to use materials that are appropriate for the age of the child. Do not include small items that may cause choking in children under 3 years old.

WHAT YOU NEED FOR BOOK CONSTRUCTION
Tracing paper or copier
1 yard yellow cotton fabric for background of pages
Heavyweight iron-on interfacing
Matching sewing thread
Gold felt scraps
Polyfil
Iron-on fusible webbing if using this method of appliqué
Scissors
Ruler
Hand and sewing machine needles
Black permanent fabric marking pen

WHAT YOU NEED FOR EACH PAGE
First Title Page: Brightly colored cotton fabric scraps; matching sewing threads; two red star beads; one small square bead.
Puppy: Brown fun-fur fabric; small pink satin scrap; red, green, white, brown and tan felt scraps; scrap of white fun fur; matching threads; ⅜-inch gold jingle bell; ivory color embroidery floss.
Flowers: Scraps of green, pink, blue, and purple felt; matching threads; scraps of rust color fabrics or felt; three yellow buttons.

Balloons: Scraps of five different-color satin fabrics; matching sewing threads; white perle cotton thread; one No. 4 large snap.

Harp: Scraps of brown and gold fabrics; matching threads; heavy cotton thread or perle cotton; decorative wooden beads.

Pocket: Scraps of denim and red sparkly fabrics; matching sewing threads; one No. 4 large snap; red embroidery floss; blank key.

Kitten: Scraps of tan fun-fur; scraps of pink flannel; scraps of white and blue felt; 22 inches of ¾-inch-wide blue satin ribbon; matching threads.

Butterfly: Scraps of green, blue, and pink sparkly fabrics; scrap of gray felt; matching sewing threads; four black glass "E" beads size 6/0; scrap pink felt; permanent black marking pen; black embroidery floss.

Lamb: Scraps of fluffy white fabric; scraps of black and white felt; black embroidery floss; matching sewing threads.

Teepee: Scraps of brown and red suede fabrics; matching sewing threads; short brown zipper; green felt fabric scrap; tan felt scrap; black embroidery floss; small piece of Velcro.

Stoplight: Scraps of red, yellow, green, and brown felt; matching sewing thread; red, yellow, and green embroidery floss; three small pieces of Velcro.

HERE'S HOW

Enlarge and trace all patterns, pages 59–61. Set aside. Prepare pages of book by cutting six pieces from the yellow cotton fabric to measure 9½×17½ inches. Cut the same number and size pieces of heavyweight interfacing. Iron interfacing onto the back of each of the six pieces of background fabric. The finished size of the open book will be 16×8 inches. Before embellishing pages with activities, lightly mark the center of each page. Each page will have two activities on it, one on the left side and one on the right side. Any embellishing and sewing is completed before assembling the pages and the book. After embellishments are completed, trim each page to measure 16½×8½ inches. Put pages right sides together and sew around outside edges using a ¼-inch seam, leaving an opening about 4 inches long to turn. Trim corners, turn pages right sides out, hand stitch openings closed, and press. Layer pages together and stitch down the center line, through all pages, over markings. For outside cover pages, insert stuffed handles in seam before sewing around side edges.

First Title Page and Back of Book: Appliqué letters and sun shape onto right side of fabric. Sew star-shape beads and small square bead to sun for eyes and nose. Use black permanent fabric marking pen to make mouth on sunshine. Leave left side of background fabric blank for the back of the book.

Puppy and Stoplight Pages: On left side of background fabric, appliqué dog body and tail fabrics in place. Outline lines with a narrow close zigzag stitch. Appliqué nose, tongue, collar, and eye pieces. Stitch ear pieces on by hand at the top of the head to leave ears floppy and free. Cut two bone pieces from light tan felt and use the buttonhole stitch and three strands of floss to stitch around outside edges. Sew floss with bone attached at puppy's mouth, leaving a length of six strands embroidery floss to dangle the bone. Sew small gold jingle bell at collar.

For the Stoplight, cut rectangle from brown felt and two circles from each of the red, yellow, and green pieces of felt. Sew rectangle to yellow background piece. Sew Velcro onto the back of one of each of the three colors of circles and onto the front of the rectangle shape. Using two strands of embroidery floss, stitch buttonhole stitches around circles to layer the two pieces of each circle color together.

Flower and Teepee Pages: Cut flower, leaf, and stem shapes from felt and two pot sections from fabric. Working on the right side of the double page, lay stems in place on the background fabric and stitch in place by sewing down center of the lengths of felt. Appliqué pot pieces over bottom ends of stems. Put leaves in place and sew down centers. Make buttonholes in centers of flower shapes. Sew buttons at ends of stems.

Cut teepee inside, top, and bottom pieces from brown suede like fabric. Cut one zigzag shape from red suede like fabric. Cut sticks from brown fabric and appliqué in place. Appliqué teepee back in place over sticks. Appliqué red zigzag design onto teepee top. Hem bottom teepee piece by turning under ¼ inch and stitching close to cut edge. Stitch zipper in teepee bottom, placing zipper top at the bottom edge and cutting off excess zipper length. Stitch teepee top to bottom using ¼-inch seam. Stitch top over back, appliquéing around sides and leaving bottom edge open. Cut 3×3½-inch piece of felted wool for inside blanket. Fold blanket up on bottom, in on the sides, and top edges down to make a baby blanket bundle shape. Tack in place with two or three hand stitches. Cut small circle for baby face out of tan felt. Make eyes, mouth, and hair in circle using black embroidery floss working French knots for eyes and stem outline stitch for mouth. Attach to blanket with two or three hand stitches. Sew Velcro pieces on the back of the blanket and to the inside back of the teepee.

Balloon and Lamb Pages: For balloons, cut four shapes from satin and appliqué in place on left side of background piece of fabric. For fifth balloon, cut two shapes from satin, leaving a ¼-inch seam allowance. Place right sides together and stitch around outside edges, leaving an opening for turning. Turn, stitch opening closed and press. Stitch lengths of perle cotton onto sides of the four balloons stitched down, tie in a knot at base of balloons and stitch through background fabric, knotting on back side. On fifth balloon, tie perle cotton thread to base of balloon and leave length of string free. Sew large snap to back of fifth balloon and onto background fabric.

For lamb, appliqué leg pieces from black felt onto right-hand side of background fabric. Appliqué fuzzy body piece over legs. Appliqué ears from black felt and head from white felt. Appliqué black felt half circle pieces for eyes and outline eyes, nose, mouth, face, and head shapes with two strands black embroidery floss.

Harp and Butterfly Pages: Appliqué harp and musical note pieces of fabric onto right-hand side of background fabric. Thread decorative beads onto thick cotton or perle cotton thread. Sew beaded threads in vertical lines in center of harp shape, knotting securely on back side of background fabric. For butterfly

wings, appliqué sparkly, glittery fabrics onto left side of background fabric. Appliqué body from gray felt, defining body sections with close zigzag appliqué stitches. Appliqué pink circle for nose. Make mouth with permanent black fabric marker. Stitch antennae using two strands black embroidery floss to make stem outline stitches. Sew two glass "E" beads at ends of antennae and two for the eyes.

Pocket and Kitten Pages: Pocket is sewn to left side of background fabric. From denim fabric cut two flap pattern pieces and one pocket piece. With right sides together, stitch side and lower edge of flap in a ¼-inch seam. Turn right side out and press. Fold straight edge of flap ¼ inch to inside. Topstitch close to all edges of flap. Turn ¼ inch under on side and lower edges of pocket and press. Turn top edge of pocket ½ inch to the inside and press. Topstitch ⅜ inch at top and close to side and lower edges. Appliqué heart shape to pocket. Sew large snap to pocket and flap. Fold flap straight edge ⅝ inch to the back and press. Stitch flap to background by sewing close to straight edge. Sew pocket under flap, stitching close to side and lower edges. Tie embroidery floss through key and stitch inside pocket.

Appliqué kitten fun-fur fabric to right-hand side of background fabric. Appliqué white and blue felt in place for eyes. Appliqué pink flannel for nose and ears. Make mouth lines by sewing small close zigzag stitches. Cut ribbon into a 2½-inch length; fold and appliqué in place at neck edge. Fold remaining length of ribbon in half and sew at neck edge.

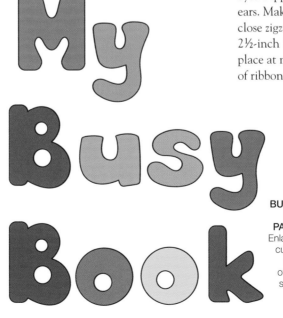

BUSY BABY BOOK PATTERNS
Enlarge 200% cut 1 each unless otherwise specified

cut 1 blue, yellow, purple, green; cut 2 red

cut 4

cut 2

BUSY BABY BOOK PATTERNS
Enlarge 200%
cut 1 each unless
otherwise specified

cut 2

cut 2

cut 2

cut 2

**BUSY BABY
BOOK
PATTERNS**
Enlarge 200%
cut 1 each unless
otherwise specified

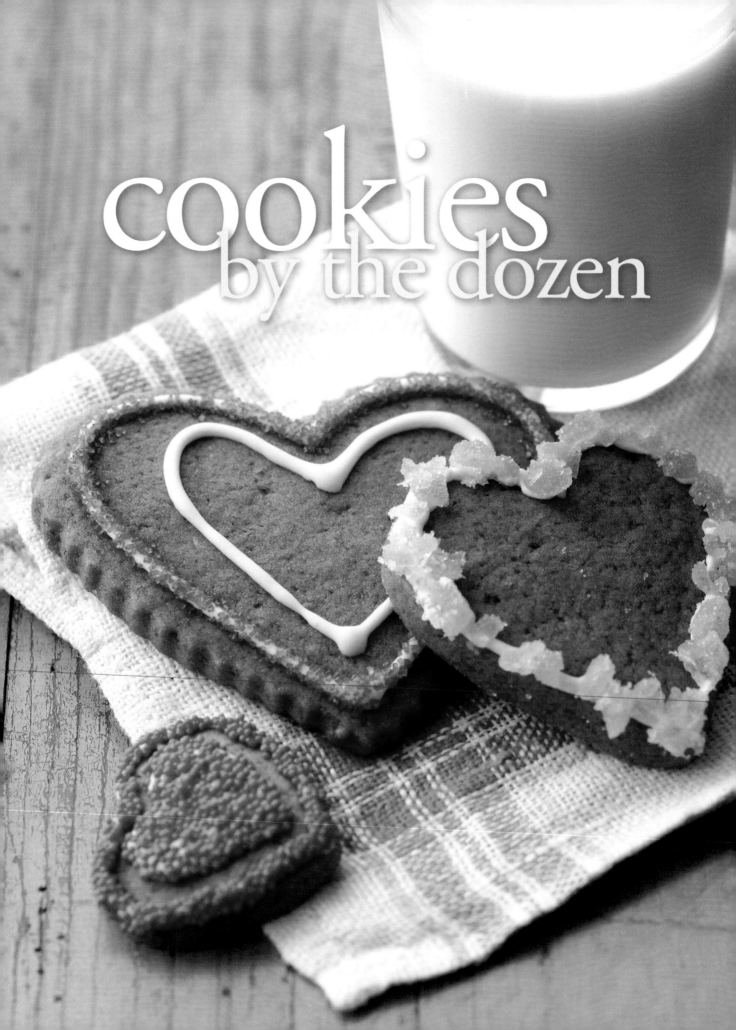

cookies
by the dozen

Whether you like them classic or contemporary, simple or showy, you will find a recipe to match your cookie-baking style.

A little bit of spice makes these two cookie recipes deliciously nice.

White Chocolate Cinnamon Wreaths, *above*, taste great with a

cup of hot tea. Santa won't be the only one who loves **Spicy Ginger**

Hearts, *opposite*, with a glass of milk. Recipes are on page 71.

Mocha—that ever-popular coffee-chocolate combo—works its magic in dessert-buffet worthy **Mocha Hazelnut Bars**, *opposite*, as well as in the more casual **Mocha Wands**, *below*. Recipes are on page 72.

Embellish these tried-and-true favorites for the holidays. Fruit and nuts add extra flavor and richness to **Cherry-Pistachio Spice Shortbread**, *opposite*. A layer of gooey goodness makes **Oatmeal-Caramel Bars**, *above*, one of the best bar cookies yet. Recipes are on pages 72–73.

The cookie tray always has room for beautiful, buttery, and fun-to-make **Spritz**, *opposite*. When you pretty them up, **Holly-Day Cookies**, *below*, can double as place cards at this year's festive dinners. Recipes are on page 74.

Good things come in small bites! That is certainly true of cute **Orange Crouton Cookie Bites,** *right*. **Butter Pecan Stars,** *below*, let you stir an all-time-favorite ice cream flavor into one great cookie. Recipes are on page 75.

Spicy Ginger Hearts
Shown on page 62

WHAT YOU NEED

- ¾ cup butter, softened
- ¾ cup packed brown sugar
- 2 tablespoons grated fresh ginger or 2 teaspoons ground ginger
- 1½ teaspoons ground black pepper
- ½ teaspoon baking soda
- ¼ teaspoon salt
- ¼ teaspoon ground cinnamon
- ¼ teaspoon ground nutmeg
- 1 egg
- ⅓ cup molasses
- 2¾ cups all-purpose flour
- 1 recipe Royal Icing or purchased decorator icing
  Red colored sugar, finely chopped crystallized ginger, and/or red nonpareils

HERE'S HOW

1. In a large mixing bowl beat butter with an electric mixer on medium to high speed for 30 seconds. Add brown sugar, ginger, pepper, baking soda, salt, cinnamon, and nutmeg. Beat until combined, scraping sides of bowl occasionally. Beat in egg and molasses until combined. Beat in as much of the flour as you can with the mixer. Stir in any remaining flour. Divide dough in half. Cover and chill for 4 to 24 hours or until dough is easy to handle.
2. Preheat oven to 350°F. Lightly grease cookie sheets or line with parchment paper; set aside.
3. On a lightly floured surface, roll half of the dough at a time until ¼ inch thick. Using heart-shape cookie cutters of various sizes, cut dough into hearts. Place cutouts about 1 inch apart on prepared

cookie sheet. (If you plan to hang the cookies on a tree as decorations, use a drinking straw to make a hole at the top of each cookie before baking.) Chill dough scraps before re-rolling.
4. Bake about 10 minutes or until tops of cookies appear dry. Cool on cookie sheet for 1 minute. Transfer cookies to wire racks and let cool. Decorate cooled cookies as desired with Royal Icing and sugar, crystallized ginger, and/or nonpareils. Makes about 48 (2-inch) cookies.
Royal Icing: In a medium mixing bowl stir together 2 cups powdered sugar and 4 teaspoons meringue powder. Add 3 tablespoons cold water. Beat with an electric mixer on low speed until combined. Beat on medium to high speed for 5 to 8 minutes or until icing is very stiff. (If mixture becomes too stiff, add more water, ½ teaspoon at a time, to make an icing of piping or spreading consistency.) If desired, divide icing into portions and tint each portion with a different paste food coloring. Decorate cookies at once with icing. Keep icing covered when not in use. Makes 2½ cups.
To store: Place undecorated cookies in an airtight container. Cover and store at room temperature for up to 2 days or freeze for up to 3 months. Thaw cookies, if frozen, and decorate as desired.

White Chocolate Cinnamon Wreaths
Shown on page 63

WHAT YOU NEED

- ¾ cup butter, softened
- ½ cup granulated sugar
- ½ cup packed brown sugar
- ½ teaspoon baking soda
- ½ teaspoon ground cinnamon
- ½ teaspoon ground ginger
- ⅛ teaspoon salt
- 1 egg
- 1 teaspoon vanilla
- 2¼ cups all-purpose flour
- 2 tablespoons granulated sugar
- 1 teaspoon ground cinnamon
  Red and/or green miniature candy-coated semisweet chocolate pieces
- 3 ounces white baking chocolate
- ½ teaspoon shortening
  Few drops green food coloring

HERE'S HOW

1. In a large mixing bowl beat butter with an electric mixer on medium to high speed for 30 seconds. Add the ½ cup granulated sugar, the brown sugar, baking soda, ½ teaspoon cinnamon, ginger, and salt. Beat until combined, scraping sides of bowl occasionally. Beat in egg and vanilla until combined. Beat in as much of the flour as you can with the mixer. Stir in any remaining flour. Divide dough in half. Cover and chill about 1 hour or until dough is easy to handle.
2. Preheat oven to 350°F. In a small bowl combine the 2 tablespoons granulated sugar and 1 teaspoon cinnamon. On a lightly floured surface, roll half of the dough at a time until ¼ inch thick. Cut with a 3-inch scalloped round cookie cutter. Cut the center from each using a 1-inch scalloped cutter. Place cutouts on an ungreased cookie sheet. Sprinkle cutouts with the sugar mixture. Carefully press candy pieces into dough.
3. Bake for 10 to 12 minutes or until edges are firm and bottoms are very light brown. Cool on cookie sheet for 2 minutes. Transfer cookies to wire racks and let cool.
4. In a small saucepan combine white chocolate and shortening. Stir over low heat just until melted and smooth. Remove from heat. Stir in food coloring to desired shade of green. Cool slightly. Place mixture in a heavy small resealable plastic bag; seal bag. Snip off a small corner of bag. Decorate cookies as desired. Makes 18 to 20 (3-inch) cookies.
To store: Layer undecorated cookies in an airtight container. Cover and store at room temperature for up to 3 days or freeze for up to 3 months. Thaw cookies, if frozen, and decorate as directed.

71

Mocha Wands
Shown on page 64

WHAT YOU NEED
- 1 cup butter, softened
- ¾ cup sugar
- 4 teaspoons instant espresso coffee powder
- ½ teaspoon salt
- ¼ teaspoon baking powder
- 1 egg
- 1 teaspoon vanilla
- 2⅓ cups all-purpose flour
- 8 ounces semisweet chocolate, melted and cooled
- 1 cup finely chopped pecans, toasted if desired

HERE'S HOW
1. Preheat oven to 375°F. In a large mixing bowl beat butter with an electric mixer on medium to high speed for 30 seconds. Add sugar, coffee powder, salt, and baking powder. Beat until combined, scraping sides of bowl occasionally. Beat in egg and vanilla. Beat in as much of the flour as you can with mixer. Stir in any remaining flour.
2. Pack dough into a cookie press fitted with a star plate. Press dough through the cookie press into 3-inch-long strips onto an ungreased cookie sheet, cutting dough from press with a small knife and spacing strips about 1 inch apart.
3. Bake for 8 to 10 minutes or until edges of cookies are firm. Transfer cookies to wire racks and let cool. Carefully dip ends of cookies into melted chocolate. Sprinkle evenly with pecans on both sides. Transfer to a waxed paper-lined cookie sheet. Let stand until chocolate is firm. Makes about 72 cookies.

To store: Layer cookies between waxed paper in an airtight container. Cover and store at room temperature for up to 3 days or freeze undipped cookies for up to 3 months. Thaw cookies, dip in melted chocolate, and sprinkle with pecans.

Mocha Hazelnut Bars
Shown on page 65

WHAT YOU NEED
- ⅓ cup butter, softened
- 1 cup packed brown sugar
- 1 cup all-purpose flour
- ½ teaspoon instant espresso coffee powder
- ½ cup finely chopped toasted hazelnuts (filberts)
- 2 eggs
- 3 tablespoons freshly brewed espresso
- 2 tablespoons all-purpose flour
- ½ teaspoon baking powder
- 1 teaspoon powdered sugar
- 1 teaspoon unsweetened cocoa powder
- Chocolate-dipped hazelnuts and/or espresso beans (optional)

HERE'S HOW
1. Preheat oven to 350°F. For crust, in a medium mixing bowl beat butter with an electric mixer on medium to high speed for 30 seconds. Beat in ¼ cup of the brown sugar until thoroughly combined. Beat in the 1 cup flour, the espresso powder, and ¼ cup of the hazelnuts until mixture is crumbly. Press mixture evenly into an ungreased 8×8×2-inch baking pan. Bake for 10 minutes.
2. Meanwhile, in a medium bowl whisk together the eggs, remaining ¾ cup brown sugar, brewed espresso, 2 tablespoons flour, and baking powder. Beat on medium speed until combined. Pour over hot crust. Sprinkle with remaining ¼ cup chopped hazelnuts.
3. Bake about 20 minutes more or until center is set. Transfer pan to a wire rack and let cool. Combine powdered sugar and cocoa powder; sprinkle over top. Cut into bars. Store bars, covered, in the refrigerator. If desired, garnish each bar with a chocolate-dipped hazelnut and/or espresso bean. Makes 16 bars.

To store: Layer bars between waxed paper in an airtight container. Cover and store in the refrigerator for up to 3 days.

Oatmeal-Caramel Bars
Shown on page 66

WHAT YOU NEED
- 1½ cups quick-cooking rolled oats
- ¾ cup all-purpose flour
- ⅔ cup packed brown sugar
- ¼ teaspoon baking soda
- ⅔ cup butter, melted
- 25 vanilla caramels
- 2 tablespoons butter
- 1 tablespoon milk
- ½ cup chopped nuts
- ⅓ cup miniature semisweet chocolate pieces

HERE'S HOW
1. Preheat oven to 350°F. Line an 8×8×2-inch baking pan with foil; set aside. In a medium bowl stir together oats, flour, brown sugar, and baking soda. Add the melted butter; stir until well combined. Set aside 1 cup of the oat mixture for topping.
2. Pat the remaining oat mixture into the foil-lined baking pan. Bake for 10 minutes.
3. Meanwhile, for filling, unwrap the caramels. In a small heavy saucepan combine caramels, the 2 tablespoons butter, and milk. Cook and stir over low heat just until melted.

4. Carefully spread filling on baked crust. Sprinkle with nuts, chocolate pieces, and reserved oat mixture. Bake about 20 minutes more or until top is golden. Transfer pan to a wire rack and let cool. Using the foil, lift out of the pan. Cut into bars. Makes 20 bars.

To store: Layer bars between waxed paper in an airtight container. Cover and store at room temperature for up to 3 days or freeze for up to 3 months.

Cherry-Pistachio Spice Shortbread

Shown on page 67

WHAT YOU NEED

2½ cups all-purpose flour
⅔ cup sugar
1 teaspoon pumpkin pie spice
1 cup butter
¼ cup snipped dried cherries
¼ cup finely chopped dry roasted pistachio nuts
2 tablespoons finely chopped dry roasted pistachio nuts
3 ounces white baking chocolate, chopped
1 teaspoon shortening

HERE'S HOW

1. Preheat oven to 325°F. Line a very large cookie sheet with parchment paper; set aside. In a large bowl combine flour, sugar, and pumpkin pie spice. Using a pastry blender, cut in butter until mixture resembles fine crumbs and starts to cling. Stir in cherries and the ¼ cup pistachio nuts. Form the mixture into a ball and knead just until smooth. Divide the dough in half.

2. Shape each dough half into a 6-inch circle on the prepared cookie sheet leaving 2 inches between the circles. If desired, make a scalloped edge around the circles. Cut each circle into 12 wedges, leaving wedges together in the circles. Sprinkle tops with the 2 tablespoons pistachio nuts. Press nuts slightly into dough.

3. Bake for 20 to 25 minutes or until bottoms just start to brown and centers are set. Cut circles into wedges again while warm. Cool on cookie sheet for 5 minutes. Transfer shortbread on the parchment paper to a wire rack and let cool.

4. In a small saucepan heat and stir white chocolate and shortening over low heat until melted and smooth. Drizzle over cooled shortbread wedges. Let stand 15 to 20 minutes or until set. Makes 24 wedges.

To store: Layer wedges without chocolate drizzle between waxed paper in airtight container. Cover and store at room temperature for up to 3 days or freeze for up to 3 months. Thaw, if frozen; drizzle with melted chocolate as directed above.

Holly-Day Cookies

When serving these cookies, if you like, write guests' names on a long ribbon of paper. Slightly curl the paper ribbon and arrange each around a cookie. Shown on page 68.

WHAT YOU NEED

- 1 cup butter, softened
- ½ cup granulated sugar
- ½ teaspoon almond extract or vanilla
- ¼ teaspoon salt
- 2½ cups all-purpose flour
- 1 tablespoon snipped fresh rosemary
- 1 recipe Creamy Lemon Frosting
- 1 recipe Sugared Cranberries
  Fresh rosemary sprigs

HERE'S HOW

1. Preheat oven to 325°F. In a large mixing bowl beat butter with an electric mixer on medium to high speed for 30 seconds. Add granulated sugar, almond extract, and salt. Beat until combined, scraping sides of bowl occasionally. Beat in as much of the flour as you can with the mixer. Stir in any remaining flour and the snipped rosemary.

2. On a lightly floured surface, roll dough until ½ inch thick. Using a lightly floured 1½-inch round cookie cutter, cut out dough. Place cutouts 2 inches apart on an ungreased cookie sheet.

3. Bake for 16 to 18 minutes or until bottoms just begin to brown. Cool on cookie sheets on wire racks for 2 minutes. Transfer cookies to wire racks and let cool.

4. To decorate cookies, spread Creamy Lemon Frosting evenly on cookie tops.

Place two Sugared Cranberries in frosting on each cookie. Pluck clusters of leaves from rosemary sprigs. Arrange a few rosemary leaf clusters around cranberries. If desired, place a name tag and a cookie on each plate. Tell guests to remove rosemary sprigs before eating cookies. Makes about 48 cookies.

Creamy Lemon Frosting: In a medium mixing bowl beat ¼ cup softened butter with an electric mixer on medium to high speed for 30 seconds. Beat in 1 tablespoon milk, ½ teaspoon finely shredded lemon peel, and 2 teaspoons lemon juice. Slowly beat in 2 cups powdered sugar, beating until mixture is smooth. Add additional milk, 1 teaspoon at a time, until frosting reaches desired consistency. Makes about ¾ cup.

Sugared Cranberries: Toss frozen cranberries with granulated sugar to coat.

To store: Layer undecorated cookies between waxed paper in an airtight container. Cover and store at room temperature for up to 3 days or freeze for up to 3 months. Thaw cookies, if frozen, and decorate as directed.

Spritz

Shown on page 69

WHAT YOU NEED

- 1½ cups butter, softened
- 1 cup granulated sugar
- 1 teaspoon baking powder
- 1 egg
- 1 teaspoon vanilla
- ¼ teaspoon almond extract
- 3½ cups all-purpose flour
- 1 recipe Powdered Sugar Icing (optional)
  Small multicolored decorative candies (optional)

HERE'S HOW

1. Preheat oven to 375°F. In a large mixing bowl beat butter with an electric mixer on medium to high speed for 30 seconds. Add sugar and baking powder. Beat until combined, scraping sides of bowl occasionally. Beat in egg, vanilla, and extract until combined. Beat in as much of the flour as you can with the mixer. Stir in any remaining flour.

2. Pack dough into a cookie press fitted with desired shaped plate. Press dough through the cookie press 2 inches apart onto ungreased cookie sheets, cutting dough from press with a small knife or metal spatula.* (To make letters as shown on page 69, use a cookie press fitted with a small star shape and press dough into desired letters.)

3. Bake for 8 to 10 minutes or until edges are firm but not brown. Transfer cookies to wire racks and let cool. If desired, trim undecorated cooled cookies with Powdered Sugar Icing and decorative candies. Makes about 84 cookies.

Powdered Sugar Icing: In a small bowl combine 1 cup powdered sugar, ¼ teaspoon vanilla, and 1 tablespoon milk. Stir in additional milk, 1 teaspoon at a time, until icing is of piping or spreading consistency. If desired, tint with food coloring. Makes ½ cup icing.

***Test Kitchen Tip:** If desired, sprinkle shapes with colored sugar or decorative candies before baking.

To store: Layer cookies between waxed paper in an airtight container. Cover and store at room temperature for up to 3 days or freeze for up to 3 months. Thaw cookies, if frozen, before serving.

Butter Pecan Stars

Shown on page 70

WHAT YOU NEED

- ½ cup butter, softened
- ⅓ cup shortening
- 1 cup packed brown sugar
- ½ teaspoon baking powder
- ¼ teaspoon baking soda
- ¼ teaspoon salt
- 1 egg
- ⅓ cup melted good-quality butter pecan ice cream
- 2¼ cups all-purpose flour
- ½ cup pecans, toasted and finely chopped
- 1 recipe Butter Pecan Icing Finely chopped toasted pecans (optional)

HERE'S HOW

1. In a large mixing bowl beat butter and shortening with an electric mixer on medium to high speed for 30 seconds. Add brown sugar, baking powder, baking soda, and salt. Beat until combined, scraping sides of bowl occasionally. Beat in egg and melted ice cream until combined. Beat in as much of the flour as you can with the mixer. Stir in any remaining flour and the ½ cup pecans. Divide dough in half. Cover and chill for 2 hours or until dough is easy to handle.
2. Preheat oven to 350°F. On a lightly floured surface, roll half of the dough at a time until about ¼ inch thick. Using 2- to 3-inch star-shaped cookie cutters, cut into stars of various sizes. Place 1 inch apart on an ungreased cookie sheet.
3. Bake for 10 to 12 minutes or until edges are set and lightly browned.

Transfer cookies to wire racks; let cool. Drizzle with Butter Pecan Icing and, if desired, sprinkle with finely chopped nuts. Makes about 36 (2½-inch) cookies.
Butter Pecan Icing: In a medium bowl stir together 1½ cups powdered sugar and 3 tablespoons melted good quality butter pecan ice cream. Add additional melted ice cream, 1 teaspoon at a time, until icing is of drizzling consistency.
To store: Layer uniced cookies between waxed paper in an airtight container. Cover and store at room temperature for up to 3 days or freeze for up to 3 months. Thaw cookies, if frozen; drizzle with icing.

Orange Crouton Cookie Bites

Shown on page 70

WHAT YOU NEED

- 1 3-ounce package cream cheese, softened (do not use reduced-fat cream cheese [Neufchâtel])
- 3 tablespoons butter, softened
- ⅔ cup granulated sugar
- ½ cup milk
- 1 egg
- 1 tablespoon finely shredded orange peel
- 1 cup all-purpose flour
- 1 teaspoon baking powder
- ½ teaspoon ground cardamom
- ¼ teaspoon salt
- 1 recipe Orange Glaze Small multicolored decorative candies

HERE'S HOW

1. Preheat oven to 350°F. Lightly grease bottom of an 8×8×2-inch baking pan.

Line bottom of pan with waxed paper or parchment paper. Grease and flour the pan; set aside.
2. In a large mixing bowl beat cream cheese and butter with an electric mixer on medium to high speed until mixture is light and fluffy. Add granulated sugar and beat until well combined; beat in milk and egg until well combined. Stir in orange peel.
3. In a small bowl stir together flour, baking powder, cardamom, and salt. Slowly beat flour mixture into cream cheese mixture until smooth. Pour batter into prepared baking pan.
4. Bake for 25 to 30 minutes or until a wooden toothpick inserted in center comes out clean. Cool in pan on a wire rack for 10 minutes. Turn out of pan and cool completely on a wire rack.
5. Cut into 1-inch cubes. Arrange, evenly spaced, on a lightly greased cookie sheet. Bake in a 350°F oven for 15 to 20 minutes or until lightly browned, turning cubes once.
6. Dip part of cooled crouton or drizzle with Orange Glaze. Sprinkle with decorative candies. To serve, place 2 or 3 croutons in paper bake or candy cups. Makes 49 to 64 bites.
Orange Glaze: In a small bowl stir together 1 cup powdered sugar and 1 teaspoon finely shredded orange peel. Stir in 4 teaspoons orange juice, 1 teaspoon at a time, until mixture is of drizzling consistency.
To store: Layer uniced cookies between waxed paper in an airtight container. Cover and store at room temperature for up to 3 days or freeze for up to 1 month. Thaw cookies, if frozen, and decorate as directed before serving.

75

perfectly
natural

Enjoy the simple elegance of the season with ideas that come from the beauty of nature.

Long pine needle cuttings and outdoor findings combine to make **Nature's Door Welcome.** The center of the wreath is filled with natural green walnuts, pistachio green Christmas balls, and pretty pinecones. The wreath is hung in bellpull style. Instructions are on page 86.

Seeds of all kinds gather together
to make a colorful **Symmetrical
Seed Ornament**, *above*. Capture
memories of the beach with a
Seashell Napkin Ring, *right*,
that can be made in minutes.

Create natural texture by layering nutshells in a **Pretty Pistachio**
Trim, *above*. The center of the trim is a simple foam egg shape.
Instructions for all of the projects are on pages 86–87.

Natural feathers of all kinds make colorful toppers for **Elegant Egg Trims**, *above*. Weave ribbon and then tuck in a pretty peacock feather for a **Natural Feather Wrap**, *opposite above*. Decorate naturally with a **Peacock Feather Swag**, *opposite below*, made with pinecones, feathers, and a teal-color sheer ribbon. Instructions for all of the projects are on pages 87–88.

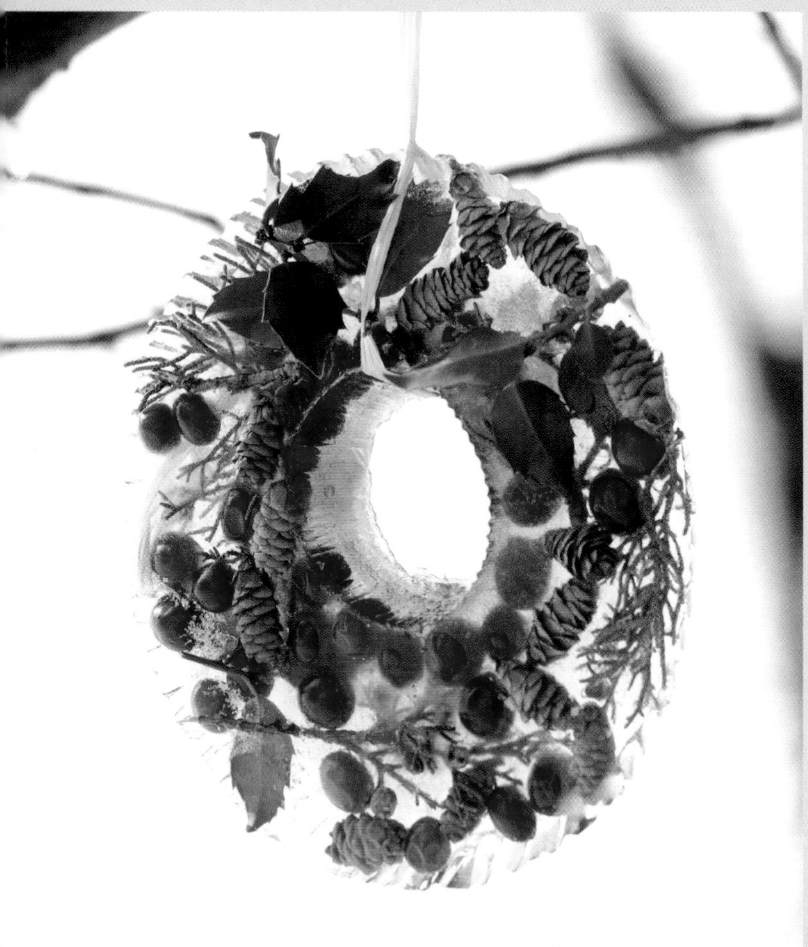

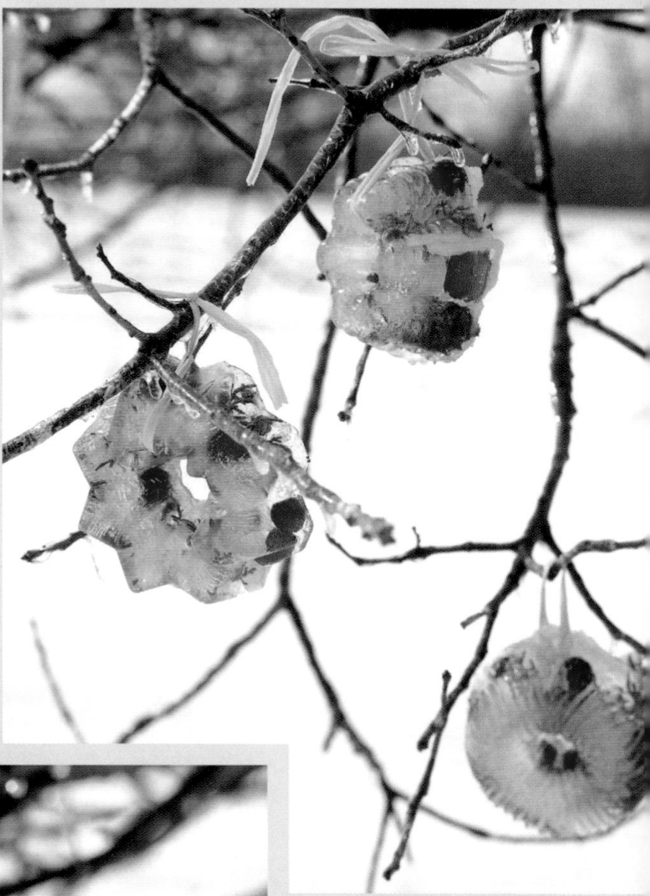

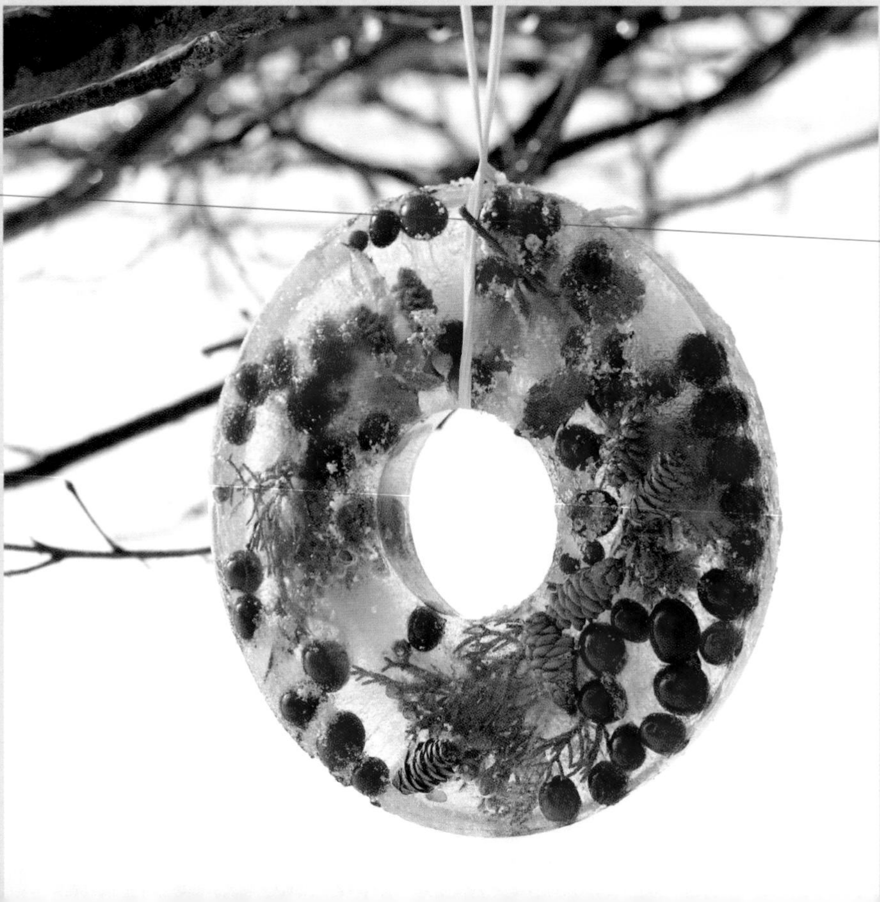

Let the sun shine through **Sparkling Ice Wreaths** to showcase nature's amazing beauty. The wreaths are created by freezing water with cranberries, pinecones, seeds, and greenery in simple baking pans. Slide the wreaths out of the pan and hang them to decorate outside trees everywhere. Nature provides the sparkle and the birds love the treats as the ice melts. Instructions are on page 88.

Make your own **Tiny Potpourri Tree**, *above*, in just a few minutes using wonderfully scented nature items. Top it off with a tiny purchased bird. Natural sunflower seeds align to make a **Sunflower Seed Wreath**, *opposite*, that can be used as an ornament or hung in a window. Instructions are on page 89.

Nature's Door Welcome

Shown on pages 76–77

WHAT YOU NEED

7-inch-diameter mounded circular
    piece of floral foam
Fresh white pine boughs
60-inch length of 6-inch-wide
    wired ribbon
3 green walnuts
Small pinecones
Glass ornaments
1 large jingle bell
1 yard twisted satin cord
Fine gold beading wire
⅜-inch dowel (6-inch long or cut to
    width of ribbon)
Scissors
Pruning shears
Hot-glue gun and glue sticks

HERE'S HOW

1. Cut pine needle clusters from branches
leaving enough stem for insertion into
floral foam. Insert into foam working
from outside into center until desired
fullness. Do not overfill center, as this is
where you will add accents.
2. Determine length of ribbon to be used.
Fold ribbon in half, wrong sides together.
3. At cut end, fold back corners on both
sides to form a point.
4. Thread beading wire through end of
jingle bell and gently twist. Leave an inch
or two to be used to fasten the bell
between the points of ribbon. Sandwich

tail of beading wire to hold bell between
points and glue points together.
5. At folded end of ribbon, glue dowel
inside fold. Slide cord ends into fold
under the dowel until the ends meet.
Glue in place. Glue edges of ribbon
together along length of each side.
6. Glue foam piece onto ribbon sash
where desired. Insert floral pins through
ribbon sash into foam to secure if desired.
7. Glue green walnuts to the center,
circle with pinecones, and add glass
ornaments to finish the piece.

Symmetrical Seed Ornament

Shown on page 78

WHAT YOU NEED

Purchased snowflake flat wood cutout
    ornament with hole for hanging
Assorted seeds: pumpkin, sunflower,
    corn, etc.
Hot-glue gun and glue sticks
Jute hanger cord

HERE'S HOW

1. Lay wood cutout on a flat surface.
Arrange seeds on wood cutout until they
cover it in a pleasing arrangement.
2. Begin gluing seeds so they optimally
cover the wood cutout. Let dry. Turn over
and cover the other side with seeds.
3. Insert hanger cord and tie.

Seashell Napkin Ring

Shown on page 78

WHAT YOU NEED

Small seashell
Crafts glue
Fine glitter
8 inches narrow ribbon

HERE'S HOW

Be sure the shell is clean and dry.
Spread a little glue on one side of the
shell and dust with glitter. Glue the
ribbon to the back of the shell and
allow to dry. Tie onto a napkin.

Pretty Pistachio Trim

Shown on page 79

WHAT YOU NEED

Medium plastic foam egg shape
    such as Styrofoam
Hot-glue gun and glue sticks
Pistachio shells
Eye pin
Bead
⅝-inch wide ribbon
Scissors; metallic gold cord

HERE'S HOW

1. Starting at narrow end of the egg form,
apply hot glue and place pistachio shells
around to form a tight bud.
2. Glue shells around egg form layer by
layer until the entire egg form is covered.

Brads/findings such as metal brad caps
or filigree pieces
Toilet paper tube cut in half
Metallic cord for hanging
Hot-glue gun and glue sticks
Scissors

HERE'S HOW
1. Eggshells should be blown out through end of egg to be decorated. Let egg dry upside down before decorating. If you do not have access to aracona eggs, dye shells with food coloring.
2. Select feathers to go with eggshell and begin trimming feathers to remove excess down or fluff for first round of feathers. Glue between one-fourth to one-third distance from end of egg with hole in it. Glue feathers around egg in tiers or rounds up to top of egg.
Note: Use a cut paper towel tube as an egg stand while working.
3. When to the top of egg, decide how to trim the egg or what finishing touches to apply. If using a bead accent on the hanging cord, apply a dab of hot glue to the base of the cord before sliding the bead down to prevent the bead from slipping off. Brads or findings such as metal bead caps or filigree pieces also add a nice finish.
Note: These ornaments store nicely in an egg carton using alternating egg cups to prevent damaging the feathers.

Some shells may fit a space better than others depending on width or "cupping" of the shell.
3. Once at the top, tie bow and insert eye pin through bead and ribbon bow. Apply some glue to pin. Insert into center top.
4. Cut gold metallic cord and thread through the eye and tie.

Elegant Egg Trims
Shown on page 80

WHAT YOU NEED
Blown out eggshells (brown, aracona, white, or dyed)
Assorted feathers (pheasant, peacock, guinea hen, turkey, or others) (available at crafts stores and online)

Natural Feather Wrap

Shown on page 81

WHAT YOU NEED

Wrapped package
½-inch-wide flat ribbon
Peacock feather
Crafts glue; scissors
Clear tape

HERE'S HOW

Cut four pieces of ribbon to fit around the wrapped package, allowing for enough ribbon to overlap in the back. Wrap two pieces of the ribbon around the box at the top of the package about 1 inch apart and glue or tape on the back. Horizontally weave the other two pieces of ribbon through the first two pieces. Glue or tape in the back. Tuck a feather into the woven area.

Peacock Feather Swag

Shown on page 81

WHAT YOU NEED

Peacock tail and body feathers
8-inch flat half-circle floral foam plastic dish, about 1-inch thick
Hot-glue gun and glue sticks
Scissors
Soft ribbon, such as Midori
Small pinecones
Floral pins

HERE'S HOW

1. Insert longest feathers on each side of foam piece with arched side up. Add additional tail feathers on each side to achieve desired fullness.
2. Glue shorter body feathers to cover any exposed floral foam.
3. Add ribbon bow and ornament accents.
4. Use a floral pin to make a hanger on back of foam.

Sparkling Ice Wreaths

Shown on pages 82–83

WHAT YOU NEED

Metal cake pans
Small custard cup or dish
Bundt cake pans
Cranberries
Pieces of greenery
Small pinecones

Holly and berries
Birdseed
Raffia

HERE'S HOW

Prepare cake pan if necessary by putting the small dish in the middle of the pan. See photo, *left.* Or use a decorative fluted tube cake pan. Arrange pieces of natural materials in the pan as desired. Fill with water. Freeze in freezer, or if weather permits, freeze outdoors. To remove wreath, dip pan in warm water. Loop raffia around the wreath and hang outside on a tree branch. As the wreath melts, birds will eat the seeds and berries.

Sunflower Seed Wreath
Shown on page 85

WHAT YOU NEED
Wreath flat wood cutout ornament
    with hole for hanging (available at
    crafts stores)
Sunflower, pumpkin, and assorted
    other seeds (available at grocery and
    garden stores)
Hot-glue gun and glue sticks
Jute hanger cord

HERE'S HOW
1. Lay wood cutout on a flat surface.
Hot glue sunflower seeds in rounds from
outside of cutout ornament into center
until cutout is covered. Work on small
sections at a time, layering seeds as
necessary to cover the wood cutout.
2. Glue accent seeds on wreath where
desired, grouping the seeds to add
interest or shape.
3. Glue on jute hanger cord.

Tiny Potpourri Tree
Shown on page 84

WHAT YOU NEED
3⅞×8⅞-inch plastic foam cone
    such as Styrofoam
Green potpourri rosettes
Artificial berry vine
Tiny pinecones
Hot-glue gun and glue sticks
Clear acrylic sealer
Tiny purchased bird

HERE'S HOW
1. Starting at the bottom of the cone
and working on a small section at a time,
spread a layer of glue over the cone.
2. Press individual potpourri rosettes
into the cone to cover entire area.
Place one large rosette on top.
3. Spray tree with clear acrylic sealer
to keep potpourri in place and to keep
it from breaking off. Wrap berry vine
around tree, gluing in place while
wrapping. Glue tiny pinecones in place
along vine.
4. Glue tiny bird to top of tree.

Fill your home with the spirit of the season with handmade projects you make yourself.

Create an entire room in a candy theme with projects that reflect the sweetness of the season. Simple peppermint candies melt together to form **Sweet Candy Trims**, *above*, that adorn your holiday tree. Instructions are on page 100. For a closer look at the projects, turn the page.

home for the
holidays

Make a variety of styles and shapes of **Sweet Candy Trims** using red-and-white and green-and-white hard candies. Adorn with tiny sprinkles and dragées to add color and detail to each piece. Instructions are on page 100.

Sew a pair of **Candy Swirl Stockings**, *left*, using bright Christmas-colored felt. Easy embroidery stitches highlight the showy candy like shapes.

Tied together with iridescent fabric, this **Soft Peppermint Pillow**, *below left*, makes a great addition to any holiday room. The pillow is stitched together and slipped over a round pillow form. Instructions are on pages 100–101.

Wire and torn fabric combine to make a **Styled Tree Napkin Holder**, *right*. These country-style napkin rings can be made in any color you like.

Tiny Snowman Place Cards, *below right*, greet each guest at the table. The little place cards with happy features are made from paper.

Spell out a seasonal greeting with a **Noel Welcome**, *opposite*, using scrapbook papers and a purchased frame. Instructions for all the projects are on pages 101–102.

Beaded Goodie Baskets, *above left,* dress up the table and hold special treats for each guest. **Santa Hat Place Cards**, *above right*, perk up any table with a jingle bell that holds the name. Stitch **Family Christmas Stockings**, *opposite*, in a style that fits each person in the house. Whether it is embroidered, tied, beaded, or quilted, each stocking has its own personality. Instructions for all of the projects are on pages 102–105.

Invite guests to their spot at the table with a simple
Pepperberry Place Card fashioned from fruit of the season,
above. Make your own sparkling snowflakes using fused
fabric and sprinkle them onto a clever **Snowflake Wreath**,
opposite, for all to enjoy. Instructions are on page 104.

Sweet Candy Trims

Shown on pages 90–92

WHAT YOU NEED

Wrapped peppermint hard candies
(red or green)
Hard decorative candies, such as
sprinkle decorations, silver dragées
Wire ornament hangers
Waxed paper
Baking sheet; oven
Hot-glue gun and glue sticks

HERE'S HOW

1. Preheat oven to 350°F. Lay waxed
paper on top of flat baking sheet. Unwrap
candies and arrange on waxed paper in
desired shape (tree, wreath, or candy
cane), making sure candies are touching.
Bake for 3 or 4 minutes, until candies are
softened a bit, watching closely so they
don't overbake and flatten (oven
temperatures vary, so experiment to assess
the right length of time for baking).
2. Remove from oven and immediately
press desired candy decorations into
softened peppermint candies. Immediately
push wire ornament hanger into the top
middle peppermint candy or glue to back
of hardened ornament. Cool and remove
from waxed paper. **Note:** These trims are
for decoration only. Do not eat.

Soft Peppermint Pillow

Shown on pages 91, 93

WHAT YOU NEED

Tracing paper; pencil; scissors
½ yard white fleece or white felt
Scraps of hot pink felt

1½ yards narrow lime green cording
1 yard iridescent white netting fabric
1¼ yard of ½-inch-wide iridescent
medium rickrack
Matching sewing threads; fabric glue
14-inch round pillow form

HERE'S HOW

1. Trace patterns, *opposite*. Set aside. Cut
two 14-inch circles from white fleece for
pillow front and back. Cut six hot pink
felt pieces from swirl pattern. Lay pink
felt pieces on top of one round white
piece of fabric, pinning in place so that
points of pink pieces almost meet in the
center. Sew around pink pieces to attach
to top of pillow. Using fabric glue attach
narrow green cording to centers of white
sections. With right sides together, sew
pillow front to pillow back, leaving an
opening to insert pillow form. Turn right
side out. Insert pillow form; hand stitch
opening closed.
2. Cut netting fabric to measure
41×36 inches. Narrowly hem the 36-inch
sides by turning under twice ¼ inch and
sewing close to fold. Center pillow
against wrong side of netting fabric and
fold under selvage edges at center back.
Cut two lengths of rickrack to measure
21 inches and tie each in a bow around
loose netting edges at sides of pillow to
resemble cellophane candy wrapping.

Candy Swirl Stockings

Shown on pages 90, 93

WHAT YOU NEED

Tracing paper or copier; pencil
Two 12×18-inch pieces of green or red

felt for stockings
One 24×24-inch piece of white felt
One 12×12-inch piece of pink or lime
green felt for candy swirls
2⅝ yard narrow lime green or pink
cording
Clear nylon sewing thread
Matching green or pink sewing thread
Fabric glue
Scissors; pinking shears

HERE'S HOW

1. Trace or copy patterns, *opposite*. Cut
two stocking pieces from background felt
color using pinking shears to cut shapes.
For each stocking, cut four white circles
from peppermint pattern on stocking.
Cut 24 pink or lime green felt pieces from
the candy swirl pattern. Using matching
sewing thread stitch swirls onto each
white felt circle. Using fabric glue secure
cording to the center of each white swirl.
Trim around outside edges of circle. Place
candies on top of stocking front at
locations marked on stocking pattern.
Pin in place.
2. Using clear nylon thread, stitch close
to outside edges through all thicknesses.
Turn stocking to back side. Use stocking
edges as a guide and trim circles to
stocking shape. Use excess circle from the
toe edge to place remaining partial circle
at top edge of stocking. With pinking
shears, cut piece of background felt to
measure ⅝×8 inches for hanging loop.
Fold length in half and place at top side
edge on the inside of stocking back. Baste
in place at top edge. With wrong sides
together stitch stocking front to back,
using a ¼-inch seam and clear nylon
sewing thread.

Styled Tree Napkin Holder
Shown on page 94

WHAT YOU NEED
1 yard cotton cording
(³⁄₁₆-inch size)
1 yard of 20 gauge
craft wire

PEPPERMINT SWIRL
Cut 6

1-inch-wide strips cotton fabric,
cut with pinking shears
Fabric glue
Decorative button, bead or bell

HERE'S HOW
Holding cording and wire together, wrap
fabric strips around tightly. Glue fabric
around cording at ends. Starting at the
bottom, lay a 3½-inch long strip of
wrapped cording flat to serve as the back
support of the tree shape. Make a bend in
the length of cording for a small loop at
the top of the tree and continue to loop
the wrapped cording around, back and
forth to make increasingly larger loops
for the tree shape, crossing over the back
vertical length of cording. End with a
2-inch-diameter circle at the bottom.
Work the end of the wrapped cording
into the tree shape. Using fabric glue,
secure the tree loops to the back vertical
support and glue the end in place. Glue
decorative item to top point.

Tiny Snowman Place Cards
Shown on page 94

WHAT YOU NEED
Tracing paper or copier; pencil
Cardstock in desired colors
¹⁄₁₆-inch thick 3-D dots
Glue stick; scissors
Purchased ornament
Extra ornament top
Fine-tip marking pen
Curtain ring

PEPPERMINT SWIRL
Cut 6

HERE'S HOW
Trace or copy patterns, page 102. From
cardstock cut out desired snowman shapes.
From the same pattern, cut out shapes to
emphasize three-dimensional pieces, such
as the scarf and hat. Stick dimensional
dots under shapes and layer on top of base
shape. Draw on features and add guest's
name. Place extra ornament top into
ornament. Place snowman in holder.
Set on curtain ring.

PEPPERMINT
STOCKING
Enlarge 400%
Cut 2

Noel Welcome

Shown on pages 90, 95

WHAT YOU NEED

Frame in desired size
Mat; cardstock; trimmer
Patterned paper and rub-ons
Oversized drawing paper
Ornament die cuts such as QuicKutz
NOEL die cut letters such as
    Accu-Cut
Ribbon
Adhesive such as Tacky Tape and
    glue dots
Die-cut machine

HERE'S HOW

1. Select a frame for the project. Consider size, color, and style. **Note:** To minimize the cost of the project, look for a frame that includes a mat. Consider frames with multiple mat openings (designed to hold several photos). You could create a wonderful wall hanging by filling those spaces with letters and embellishments. If necessary, order a custom mat to match the project at a frame shop.
2. Select patterned paper for this project, then choose cardstock to match. Select matching ribbon and snowflake rub-ons or stickers. **Note:** Be sure to choose flat embellishments so the completed project will fit back into the frame.
3. From the large sheet of drawing paper, cut a piece the size of the mat. This is the base of the project to which everything else is adhered. Adhere the drawing paper

to the back side of the mat using strong double-sided adhesive.
4. Die-cut the word NOEL using a large font. Measure the width of the word and cut a piece of cardstock to fit behind it in the mat opening and adhere. Cut a piece of patterned paper to fill the remaining space in the mat opening and adhere.
5. Cut a narrow strip of paper and adhere vertically along the border between the patterned paper and cardstock.
6. Center and adhere the word NOEL to the cardstock.
7. Die cut three ornaments (or use stickers) and adhere to the patterned paper as desired.
8. Cut short lengths of narrow ribbon and adhere vertically above each ornament. Knot short pieces of ribbon and adhere to the ornament tops using glue dots.
9. Add rub-on snowflakes to the ornaments and NOEL as desired. Place completed project in frame.

Beaded Goodie Baskets

Shown on page 96

WHAT YOU NEED

Pencil; marking pen
Bowl or other circle shape
Large paper plate
Two 7-inch squares of fabric for
    each basket
Pinking shears
Foam paintbrush
White crafts glue
Liquid starch
Jar or glass
Rubber band
Awl
24-gauge wire
Beads in desired colors

HERE'S HOW

1. Trace around a cereal bowl or other circle shape onto the back of two pieces of fabric. Cut out with pinking shears.
2. Working on a paper plate, brush the back of one circle with white glue. Adhere the two pieces together by placing the circles wrong sides together. Brush on a coat of liquid starch over both sides of the double-layer fabric circle.
3. Center the layered circles over the bottom of a jar or glass and form the circles to the curve. Hold in place with a rubber band. Fluff out the edges of the circle to distribute the gathers evenly. Let the basket dry for several hours. Remove basket from the jar.
4. Poke holes on opposite sides of basket using awl. Thread the wire through the holes twisting and adding beads as desired.

Santa Hat Place Cards

Shown on page 96

WHAT YOU NEED

Tracing paper or copier; pencil
Square of stiff red glitter felt
Scrap white fluffy, furry fabric
Fabric glue
Needle, red sewing thread
Straight pins; scissors
20-mm gold jingle bell

HERE'S HOW

Trace pattern, *opposite*, using tracing paper or copier. Place pattern on red glitter felt and cut out one shape for each holder. Cut 1½×8-inch piece of white fabric. Fold long edges under ¼ inch and glue to back side of fabric to make a strip 1×8 inches. Glue white trim in place on front lower curved edge of red felt. Match straight edges of red felt wrapping them around and making a cone shape. Pin

TINY SNOWMAN PLACECARDS
Full-Size Patterns

straight edges together and stitch with a tight whipstitch using matching red thread. Sew large jingle bell firmly to top point, using matching red thread. Slide place card through top bell slit.

Family Christmas Stockings
Shown on page 97

WHAT YOU NEED

Tracing paper or copier; pencil
Scraps of red fabric for stockings
Scraps of assorted fabrics (cotton, felt, crushed velour) for cuffs
Matching threads
One 2×7-inch strip of fabric
For embroidered cuff: Red metallic embroidery floss, green embroidery floss, three 6-mm red jingle bells
Marking pen
For quilted cuff: Red metallic sewing thread
For beaded cuff: Assorted decorative glass beads
For ribbon cuff: 1¾ yards of 2½-inch-wide red satin ribbon
For angled cuff: Decorative brooch, button, or large jingle bell

HERE'S HOW

1. For each stocking, trace and cut stocking and cuff patterns, page 105. Cut two stocking pieces from red fabric. With right sides together, sew stocking pieces along side and lower edges using a ¼-inch seam allowance. Clip curves; turn right side out; press.
2. For loop, fold long edges right sides together and stitch using ¼-inch seam. Turn right side out. Fold in half with top raw edges even. Place loop inside stocking at top edge, with loop hanging down inside stocking. Baste in place at side edge of stocking.

For ribbon cuff:
If fabric ravels, turn under top raw edge of stocking and stitch across top to hem top raw edge. Attach hanging loop at side edge and stitch through stocking at side seam. Cut piece of ribbon 13 inches long and wrap around top edge of stocking, starting and stopping at the center back of the stocking. Fold under raw edge and overlap over starting end. Stitch through ribbons at fold and at top close to edge and through stocking top. Cut remaining ribbon length into two pieces. Place right side cut edges of ribbons at side seams of stocking 1 inch from the top edge with ribbons extending to the back of the stocking.

Stitch along side edges of stocking, close to cut edge of ribbon. Flip ribbons to the front and tie into a bow. Angle cut bottom edges of ribbon.

For beaded cuff:
If using felt for cuff, cut one cuff piece from pointed pattern, placing side along fold. With right sides together sew side seam with a ¼-inch seam. If using other fabric, cut two pieces to line the cuff. Fold hanging loop in half and place inside stocking at side edge, having top raw edges at top edge of stocking; baste in place. Insert cuff inside stocking with right side of cuff to the wrong side of stocking and having top raw edges even. Stitch top seam in a ⅜-inch seam to attach cuff to stocking. Flip cuff to outside and lightly press top edge.

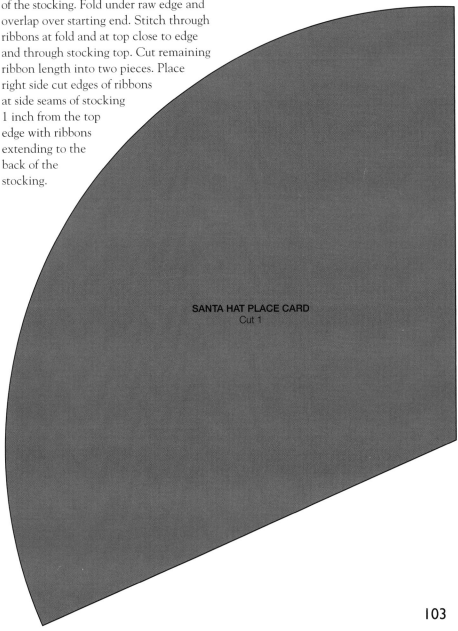

SANTA HAT PLACE CARD
Cut 1

home for the holidays

Using two strands of sewing thread or heavy upholstery thread, sew decorative beads at points of cuff.

For embroidered cuff:
Cut two cuff pieces from straight-edge pattern, placing side edges on fold. On one cuff section, mark design to be embroidered. Using four strands red metallic embroidery thread, stitch letters using running stitch. Using two strands green embroidery thread stitch lines of holly leaves using stem outline stitch. Sew jingle bells at leaf centers. With right sides together stitch side edges of cuff front using ¼-inch seams. Stitch side edges of cuff lining. With right sides together, place lining tube inside cuff and stitch along lower edge using a ¼-inch seam. Turn right side out and press lower edge. Fold hanging loop in half and place inside stocking at side edge, having top raw edges at top edge of stocking; baste in place. Insert cuff inside stocking, with right side of cuff to the wrong side of stocking and having top raw edges even. Stitch top seam in a ⅜-inch seam to attach cuff to stocking.

For quilted cuff:
Cut two pieces from scalloped edged cuff pattern, placing side edges at fold. With right sides together, stitch side edge of cuff front and side edge of cuff lining, using ¼-inch seams. With right sides together, place lining tube inside cuff and stitch along lower edge in a ¼-inch seam. Clip curves; turn right side out and press lower edge. Using metallic sewing thread, machine-quilt free design through both cuff and cuff lining. Fold hanging loop in half and place inside stocking at side edge, having top raw edges at top edge of stocking; baste in place. Insert cuff inside stocking, with right side of cuff to the wrong side of stocking and having top raw edges even. Stitch top in a ⅜-inch seam to attach cuff to stocking.

For angled cuff:
Cut two pieces from angled cuff pattern, placing side edges at fold. With right sides together, stitch side edges of cuff front. Stitch side edges of cuff lining. With right sides together, place lining tube inside cuff and stitch along lower edge in a ¼-inch seam. Turn right side out and press lower edge. Fold hanging loop in half and place inside stocking at side

edge, having top raw edges at top edge of stocking; baste in place. Insert cuff inside stocking, with right side of cuff to the wrong side of stocking and having top raw edges even. Stitch top using a ⅜-inch seam to attach cuff to stocking. Using matching thread, take a few large gathering stitches from bottom edge of stocking to top edge at short side of cuff. Pull up stitches to gather where decorative brooch, button, or large jingle bell can be placed.

Pepperberry Place Card
Shown on page 98

WHAT YOU NEED
Pepperberries
Ferns
Narrow ribbon; white glue
Small name tag

HERE'S HOW
Cinch together delicate sprigs of pepperberries and ferns with a pretty ribbon. Create a simple name tag and glue the ribbon to the petite name tag. Set on the plate.

Snowflake Wreath
Shown on page 99

WHAT YOU NEED
Tracing paper or copier; pencil
White or cream-colored heavy decorative paper
Scraps of iron-on stabilizer such as Pellon brand Peltex #72 double-sided fusible ultrafirm stabilizer
White glue
Iridescent glitter

5-mm crystal sequins
Scissors
Awl
Fine wire
Fresh evergreen wreath
Pinecones

HERE'S HOW
Trace pattern, *below,* using tracing paper or copier. Sandwich stabilizer between wrong sides of paper pieces. Fuse to paper. Place pattern onto paper and draw around pattern lightly with pencil. Cut out shapes. Add additional detail to shapes by making designs with white glue, sprinkling on iridescent glitter and adding sequins. When glue is dry make a hole through the edge of each snowflake by poking with an awl or sharp point of scissors. Add a wire to each snowflake. Wire onto the wreath. Add pinecones and other embellishments as desired.

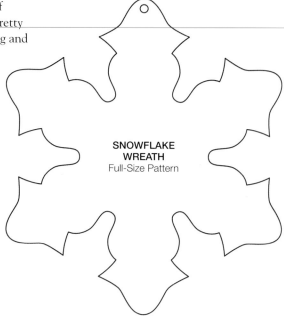

SNOWFLAKE WREATH
Full-Size Pattern

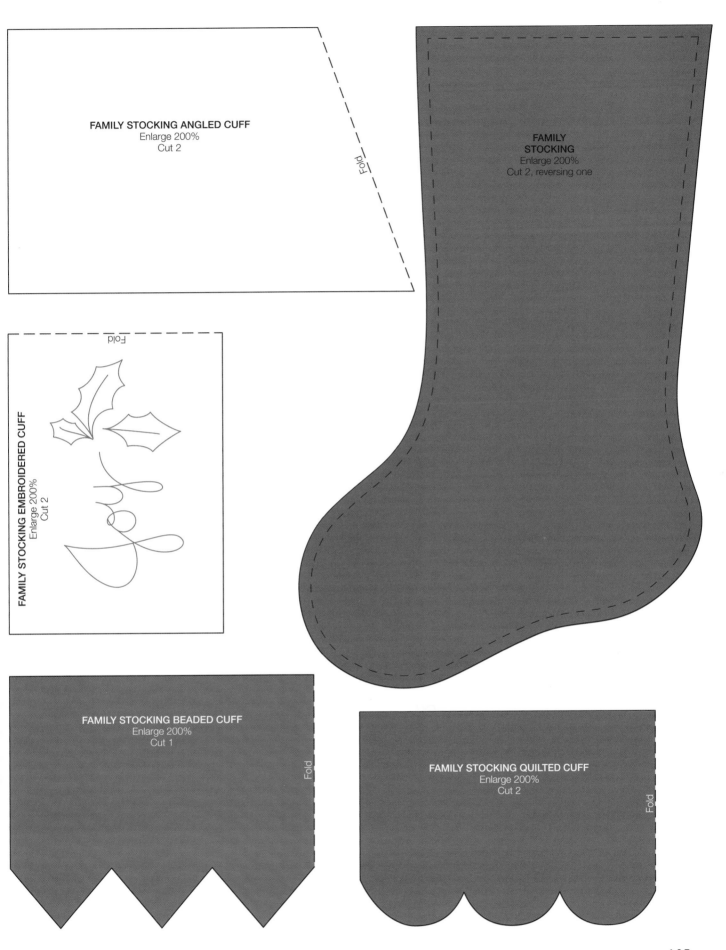

FAMILY STOCKING ANGLED CUFF
Enlarge 200%
Cut 2

Fold

FAMILY STOCKING
Enlarge 200%
Cut 2, reversing one

FAMILY STOCKING EMBROIDERED CUFF
Enlarge 200%
Cut 2

Fold

FAMILY STOCKING BEADED CUFF
Enlarge 200%
Cut 1

Fold

FAMILY STOCKING QUILTED CUFF
Enlarge 200%
Cut 2

Fold

*Keep it simple this year with ideas
you can make in the blink of an eye!*

·in the
nick of time

Sparkling clear candlesticks and vintage

ornaments gather together to make a **Simple**

Ornament Display. Choose candlesticks of

different heights and ornaments of varying

sizes to make the display shine at all levels.

Instructions are on page 116.

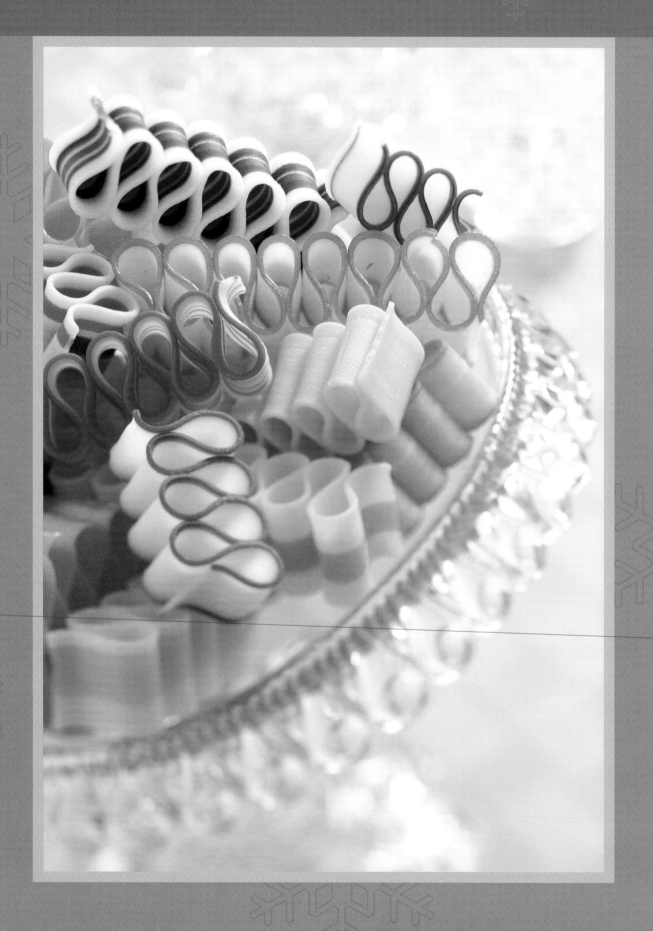

Use the vibrant colors and texture that a favorite old-fashioned candy provides to make **Ribbon Candy Fun** *opposite*. Choose a clear glass bowl and then arrange the candy sweetly in the dish.

Rummage around in the back of the cupboard for an interesting container to transform into a **Carnation Snowball Centerpiece**, *above*. Here an old silver trophy serves as a sophisticated perch for a florist's foam ball covered in white carnations. Tendrils of ivy cascade down the sides of the trophy for an added touch of elegance. Instructions are on page 116.

Use a favorite Christmas snack to make clever centerpieces in no
time. Choose unpopped or popped popcorn to surround a favorite
candle creating **Quick Popcorn Candles**, *left*.

Try a new, inventive use for tree ornaments by turning them
into delightful **Ornament Vases**, *above*. Choose mercury balls
because they are more durable than glass balls and have a lovely
shine. Instructions are on pages 116–117.

It is never too late to make a special gift for a favorite friend. Create some **Last-Minute Giveaways** in less than 10 minutes! Wrap bars of a favorite soap in bright red paper and add a sticker. Fill a simple jar with purchased gingerbread cookies and tie with a colorful bow. Or purchase some festive Christmas stamps and tuck them into a clear ornament. Instructions are on page 117.

Fill a vintage coffee cup with tiny ornaments to make a **Cup of Sparkle**, *above*. Use the colorful container as a mini-centerpiece or place on a small table with little gifts.

Create a **Pretty Poinsettia Banister**, *opposite*, in just a few minutes with evergreen clippings and blooms from a poinsettia plant. Simply snip off the blooms and keep them fresh in water tubes while they adorn evergreen on the banister. Instructions are on page 117.

Simple Ornament Display
Shown on pages 106—107

WHAT YOU NEED
Clear candlesticks in different heights
Vintage ornaments in different sizes

HERE'S HOW
Be sure the candlesticks are clean and
dry. Use window cleaner if necessary
to make them sparkle. Arrange the
candlesticks varying the heights. Place
the ornaments on top of the candlesticks
as desired.

Ribbon Candy Fun
Shown on page 108

WHAT YOU NEED
Low clear glass dish or bowl
Ribbon candy

HERE'S HOW
Be sure the dish is clean and dry. Remove
the candy from the box and arrange by
randomly layering the candy in the dish.
Note: If some of the fragile candy is
broken, use these pieces as well,
positioning the smaller pieces to give
height and interest to the arrangement.

Carnation Snowball Centerpiece
Shown on page 109

WHAT YOU NEED
Small silver container
Round oasis floral ball
Bowl or dish
Water
Scissors
2 to 3 dozen small white carnations
Fresh ivy

HERE'S HOW
1. Polish the container and set aside.
2. Fill the bowl or dish with water and
soak the ball in the bowl or dish until
it is thoroughly saturated.
3. Using scissors cut off the carnation
heads. Insert carnations to completely
cover the surface of the floral ball.
Place the carnation-filled ball into the
container. Add more water if necessary.
4. Poke the ivy between the carnation-
covered ball and the container edge.
The arrangement will keep for about
4 days.

Quick Popcorn Candles
Shown on page 110

**WHAT YOU NEED FOR THE
UNPOPPED CANDLE CENTERPIECE**
Clear glass square dish
Unpopped colored popcorn
Square cream-color candle

**WHAT YOU NEED FOR THE POPPED
CANDLE CENTERPIECE**
Clear glass round dish or bowl
White popped corn
Red pillar candle

HERE'S HOW
Place the candle in the center of the dish.
Fill the dish with the popcorn around the
candle. **Note:** Do not eat the popcorn
after it has been used for the centerpieces.
Never leave a burning candle unattended.

Ornament Vases
Shown on page 111

WHAT YOU NEED
Mercury ball ornaments
Metal file
Small terra-cotta flowerpots to
    fit the balls
Silver spray paint; flowers

HERE'S HOW
1. Pull the hangers from the tops of the
mercury balls and use a metal file to make
the tops smooth. See photo A, *opposite.*
Set aside.
2. Spray paint the flower pots. Let dry.

3. Place the balls into the flower pot. Fill the balls with water. See photo B, *above.* Add tulips or other flowers. If desired, tuck in bits of bent greenery or twigs to hold the flowers upright.

Last-Minute Giveaways
Shown on pages 112–113

WHAT YOU NEED FOR THE COOKIE JAR
Purchased clear glass jar (available at discount stores)

Purchased cookies such as gingerbread cookies
Ribbon; gift tag

HERE'S HOW
Wash and dry the jar. Fill with cookies. Put lid on jar; add ribbon and tag.

WHAT YOU NEED FOR THE STAMPS IN ORNAMENT
Clear glass ornament (available at crafts stores)
Christmas postage stamps
Narrow ribbon

HERE'S HOW
Take the top off the ornament. Roll the stamps and place in the ornament. Replace ornament top. String a ribbon through the hanger.

WHAT YOU NEED FOR THE GIVEAWAY SOAPS
Favorite bar of soap (those with square corners work best)
Wrapping paper; ribbon
Stickers

HERE'S HOW
Wrap the soap as if wrapping a package. Add a ribbon and sticker. Add tag if desired.

Cup of Sparkle
Shown on page 114

WHAT YOU NEED
Clear patterned glass coffee cup and saucer
Small ornaments

HERE'S HOW
Be sure the cup is clean and dry. Fill with ornaments, arranging so colors are randomly mixed throughout the cup.

Pretty Poinsettia Banister
Shown on page 115

WHAT YOU NEED
Pieces of evergreen
Fine wire
Small poinsettia plant with stems that fit into floral tubes
Scissors
Dish of water
Small floral tubes (available at floral shops)

HERE'S HOW
Wire the evergreens to the banister as desired. Clip the poinsettia blooms from the plant and put in the dish of water. One at a time, place the blooms into the floral tubes; place into the greens as desired. **Note:** Depending on the plants, replace the water in the tubes as necessary.

celebrate with chocolate

You can always count on chocolate to win some "wows." These ten irresistible recipes call on this all-time-favorite ingredient in holiday-worthy ways.

Airy in texture but rich in flavor, **Chocolate Mousse with Raspberry Sauce,** *above,* offers lusciousness by the spoonful. A candy-bar filling makes for one sweet surprise in **Brownie Surprise Cupcakes,** *opposite.* Recipes are on page 127.

There is no need to turn on the oven for **Coffee-Mallow Torte**, *above*. Simply stir, spread, and pour your way to an irresistible frozen dessert. **Chocolate-Glazed Honey Walnut Tart**, *opposite*, is so rich you should serve it in thin slices. But don't be surprised if everyone asks for seconds! Recipes are on pages 127–128.

A few dollops of airy topping and some chocolate shavings make

Merry Mocha Pound Cake, *below*, a fitting holiday-feast finale.

When you want to pull out all the stops, set your sights on glamorous

Chocolate-Spice Harvest Fruit-Topped Cake, *opposite*. Recipes

are on pages 128–129.

With two kinds of nuts, two kinds of chocolate, and candied orange peel, **Triple-Orange Nutty Fudge**, *above*, deserves a place in the Holiday Fudge Hall of Fame. Pass a tray of **Fudge Brownie Tassies**, *opposite*, for a small but hugely satisfying dessert. Recipes are on pages 129–130.

Choose **Chocolate-Mint Ice Cream**, *right*, for a cool and refreshing finish to a holiday meal. For something richer and more decadent, serve **Chocolate-Peppermint Pie**, *above*. Both combine chocolate and mint in scrumptious ways. Recipes are on pages 130–131.

Chocolate Mousse with Raspberry Sauce

Shown on page 119

Coffee-Mallow Torte

Shown on page 120

Brownie Surprise Cupcakes

Shown on page 118

- 1 18.3- to 21-ounce package fudge brownie mix
- 15 miniature-size chocolate-coated caramel-topped nougat bars with peanuts
- 1 16-ounce can vanilla frosting
  Maraschino cherries and/or chopped chocolate-coated caramel-topped nougat bars with peanuts (optional)

1. Preheat oven to 350°F. Line fifteen 2½-inch muffin cups with paper bake cups. Prepare the fudge brownie mix according to package directions. Spoon 1 tablespoon of the batter into each paper bake cup. Place a miniature-size candy bar in each cup. Divide the remaining batter among the cups.

2. Bake for 22 minutes.* Let cool in pans on a wire rack. Cupcakes may dip slightly in center. Frost with vanilla frosting and, if desired, top with maraschino cherries and/or chopped chocolate-coated caramel-topped nougat bars with peanuts. Makes 15 cupcakes.

***Test Kitchen Tip:** If all of the cupcakes do not fit in the oven at one time, refrigerate the unbaked extras until the first cupcakes finish baking.

- ¾ cup raspberry jam
- 1 tablespoon raspberry liqueur or orange juice
- 3 ounces semisweet chocolate
- 1 ounce bittersweet chocolate
- 2 tablespoons honey
- 1 tablespoon brandy or orange juice
- 2½ cups whipping cream
  Chocolate curls* or grated chocolate

1. In a small saucepan heat jam over low heat until melted, stirring occasionally. Remove from heat. Stir in raspberry liqueur; set aside to cool completely.

2. In another small saucepan heat chocolates over low heat until melted and smooth. Remove from heat. Stir in honey, brandy, and 1 tablespoon of the whipping cream until well combined. Transfer mixture to a large bowl; set aside to cool completely.

3. In a chilled large mixing bowl beat remaining cream until stiff peaks form. Set aside 1 cup of the whipped cream. Stir ½ cup whipped cream into chocolate mixture to lighten. Fold remaining whipped cream into chocolate mixture.

4. Spoon the chocolate mixture into 6 wineglasses or dessert dishes. Top with reserved whipped cream. Spoon cooled raspberry sauce over whipped cream and top with chocolate curls. Cover and chill for 1 to 6 hours. Makes 6 servings.

***Test Kitchen Tip:** For chocolate curls, slowly draw a vegetable peeler across the edge of a bar of semisweet or milk chocolate. It works best if the chocolate is at room temperature.

- 2 cups crushed chocolate wafer cookies (about 35 cookies)
- ⅓ cup butter, melted
- ⅔ cup hot fudge ice cream topping
- 1 teaspoon instant coffee crystals
- ½ of a 7-ounce jar marshmallow crème
- 1 8-ounce container frozen whipped dessert topping, thawed
- 1 quart coffee ice cream
- ⅓ cup chopped pecans, toasted
- ½ ounce semisweet chocolate, grated
- ⅓ cup caramel-flavored ice cream topping
- ¼ ounce semisweet chocolate, shaved
  Pecan halves (optional)

1. In a medium bowl combine cookie crumbs and butter. Press into the bottom and about 1½ inches up the sides of a 9-inch springform pan; set aside.

2. In a small saucepan combine hot fudge topping and coffee crystals. Heat and stir just until smooth; cool slightly. Spread fudge topping over the crumb mixture in the springform pan. In a large bowl fold marshmallow crème into whipped dessert topping until combined; set aside.

3. In a chilled large bowl stir ice cream with a wooden spoon until softened. Fold in whipped topping mixture. Spoon into crust. Sprinkle with chopped pecans and grated chocolate. Cover and freeze for 6 hours or until firm. Before serving, let stand at room temperature for 10 minutes. Drizzle with caramel topping and sprinkle with shaved chocolate. If desired, garnish with pecan halves. Makes 12 to 16 servings.

Chocolate-Glazed Honey Walnut Tart

For easier cutting and to prevent the chocolate layer from cracking, run hot water over the knife blade and wipe it dry. Shown on page 121.

- 1¼ cups all-purpose flour
- ¼ cup granulated sugar
- ½ cup cold butter
- 1 egg yolk, lightly beaten
- 3 tablespoons cold water
- 3 eggs, lightly beaten
- ½ cup honey
- ½ cup light-colored corn syrup
- ½ cup packed brown sugar
- ⅓ cup butter, melted
- 1 teaspoon vanilla
- 2 cups chopped walnuts, toasted
- ¾ cup semisweet chocolate pieces
- ⅓ cup butter
- 1 tablespoon light-colored corn syrup

1. In a medium bowl stir together flour and granulated sugar; cut in ½ cup butter until pieces are the size of small peas. In a small bowl stir together egg yolk and cold water. Gradually stir yolk mixture into flour mixture just until moistened. Gently knead the dough just until a ball forms. Cover with plastic wrap; chill for 1 to 2 hours or until dough is easy to handle.

2. Preheat oven to 350°F. Using your hands, flatten dough on a lightly floured surface. Roll dough from center to edges, forming a 13-inch circle. Wrap pastry around the rolling pin. Unroll pastry into an 11-inch tart pan with a removable bottom. Ease pastry into pan; avoid stretching pastry. Press pastry into the fluted sides of pan. Trim pastry even with edge of pan. Do not prick pastry.

3. For filling, in a large mixing bowl combine 3 eggs, honey, ½ cup corn syrup, brown sugar, ⅓ cup melted butter, and vanilla. Mix well. Stir in nuts.

4. Place the pastry-lined tart pan on a baking sheet on the oven rack. Carefully pour filling into pan. Bake for 40 minutes or until a knife inserted near the center comes out clean. Cool on a wire rack for 1 hour.

5. Meanwhile, for chocolate glaze, in a heavy medium saucepan heat and stir the chocolate, ⅓ cup butter, and 1 tablespoon corn syrup over low heat until melted and smooth. Remove from heat. Transfer mixture to a small bowl. Cover and chill for 20 to 30 minutes or until mixture is thickened slightly, stirring occasionally. Spoon and spread thickened glaze over the top of the tart. Chill for 1 hour or until set. To serve, cut into wedges. Store, covered, in the refrigerator for up to 3 days. Makes 16 servings.

Chocolate-Spice Harvest Fruit-Topped Cake

Shown on page 122

- 1 8-ounce carton dairy sour cream
- 1 cup water
- ⅔ cup canola oil
- 2 cups sugar
- 2 eggs
- 1 teaspoon vanilla
- 2 teaspoons baking powder
- ½ teaspoon baking soda
- ½ teaspoon salt
- 2 cups all-purpose flour
- ¾ cup unsweetened cocoa powder
- ¾ teaspoon freshly ground black pepper
- ½ teaspoon ground cinnamon
- ½ teaspoon ground allspice
- ½ teaspoon ground nutmeg
- ⅛ teaspoon ground cloves
- 1 cup whipping cream
- 8 ounces semisweet chocolate, finely chopped
- 1 recipe Fruit Topping
- ⅔ cup caramel-flavored ice cream topping (optional)

1. Preheat oven to 350°F. Grease and flour two 9×1½-inch round cake pans; set aside.

2. In a very large bowl combine sour cream, water, oil, sugar, eggs, vanilla, baking powder, baking soda, and salt. Whisk until well combined. Add flour, cocoa powder, black pepper, cinnamon, allspice, nutmeg, and cloves; whisk vigorously until smooth. Divide batter between prepared pans.

3. Bake for 30 to 35 minutes until top springs back when lightly touched in centers. Cool in pans on wire racks for 10 minutes. Remove cake layers from pans and cool completely.

4. In a medium saucepan bring whipping cream to boiling over medium-high heat. Remove from heat and stir in semisweet chocolate until smooth. Cool to room temperature. Chill until spreadable, about 1 hour. Meanwhile, prepare Fruit Topping.

5. To assemble, place a cake layer on a serving plate. Spread with half of the chocolate-cream mixture. Top with the second cake layer. Spread with remaining chocolate-cream mixture. Arrange fruit in a single layer on top of cake. If using, pour ice cream topping over the fruit. Serve immediately with any remaining fruit. (Cake does not store well after fruit is added.) Makes 12 servings.

Fruit Topping: Thinly slice 1 unpeeled pear lengthwise and 1 unpeeled cooking apple horizontally. In a medium saucepan combine 2 cups apple juice and 1 cup sugar; bring to boiling over medium-high heat. Add sliced pear, apple, and ⅓ cup dried cranberries; return to boiling. Reduce heat. Simmer, covered, for 2 minutes. Remove from heat and let stand for 5 minutes. Strain; discard liquid. Cool fruit mixture to room temperature.

Merry Mocha Pound Cake

Shown on page 123

- ⅔ cup butter, softened
- 2 cups all-purpose flour
- 1¼ cups granulated sugar
- ½ teaspoon salt
- ½ teaspoon cream of tartar
- ¼ teaspoon baking soda
- 1 tablespoon instant coffee crystals
- ½ cup cold water
- 1 teaspoon vanilla
- 3 eggs
- 2 ounces unsweetened chocolate, melted and cooled
- 1 recipe Coffee Cream
  Milk chocolate curls
  Instant coffee crystals

1. Preheat oven to 325°F. Grease and flour a 9×5×3-inch loaf pan; set aside. In a large mixing bowl beat butter with an electric mixer on medium to high speed for 30 seconds. In a medium bowl combine flour, sugar, salt, cream of tartar, and baking soda. Add flour mixture to butter; beat for 2 to 3 minutes or until mixture forms fine crumbs.

2. In a small bowl dissolve the 1 tablespoon coffee crystals in the cold water. Add coffee mixture and vanilla to beaten mixture; beat on low speed until combined. Beat for 2 minutes more on medium speed. Add eggs and melted chocolate; beat on low speed until well mixed. Beat for 1 minute more on medium speed.

3. Pour into prepared loaf pan. Bake for 75 to 80 minutes or until a wooden toothpick inserted near the center comes out clean. Cool in pan on a wire rack for 10 minutes. Remove from pan. Cool completely on wire rack. To serve as shown, cut slices in half and layer with Coffee Cream, chocolate curls, and additional coffee crystals. Serves 10 to 12.

Coffee Cream: In a medium mixing bowl stir 1 tablespoon powdered sugar and 1 teaspoon instant coffee crystals into 1 cup whipping cream. Chill for 10 minutes. Beat with an electric mixer on medium speed until stiff peaks form.

Triple-Orange Nutty Fudge

Shown on page 124

- 3 cups sugar
- 1 12-ounce can evaporated milk
- 4 tablespoons butter
- 1½ cups milk chocolate pieces
- ¾ cup chopped walnuts
- ½ teaspoon vanilla
- ¼ teaspoon orange extract
- 1½ cups white baking pieces
- ¾ cup chopped dry roasted pistachio nuts
- ½ teaspoon vanilla
- ¼ teaspoon orange extract
- 1 recipe Candied Orange Peel, chopped
- 1 recipe Dark Chocolate-Orange Glaze

1. Line a 9×9×2-inch baking pan with foil, extending the foil over the edges of the pan. Butter foil; set aside.

2. In a 2-quart heavy saucepan combine 1½ cups of the sugar, ¾ cup of the evaporated milk, and 2 tablespoons of the butter. Cook and stir over medium heat until boiling. Continue to boil at a moderate, steady rate for 3 minutes, stirring frequently. Remove from heat. Stir in the milk chocolate pieces, walnuts, ½ teaspoon vanilla, and ¼ teaspoon orange extract until chocolate is completely melted. Pour into prepared pan. Cover and chill while preparing white layer.

3. In a clean 2-quart heavy saucepan combine remaining sugar, evaporated milk, and butter. Cook and stir over medium heat until boiling. Continue

to boil at a moderate, steady rate for 3 minutes, stirring frequently. Remove from heat. Stir in the white baking pieces, pistachio nuts, ½ teaspoon vanilla, and ¼ teaspoon orange extract until chocolate is completely melted.

4. Pour white chocolate mixture evenly over milk chocolate mixture in pan. Top immediately with chopped Candied Orange Peel. Drizzle with Dark Chocolate-Orange Glaze. Cover and chill for 4 hours or until firm.

5. When fudge is firm, use foil to lift it out of pan. Cut fudge into about 1-inch pieces. Store, covered, in the refrigerator up to 1 week. Makes about 3¼ pounds (about 64 pieces).

Candied Orange Peel: Cut peels of 2 oranges lengthwise into quarters, cutting just through the pulp to the surface of the fruit. Pry back the quartered peel using the back of a spoon. Using the bowl of the spoon, scrape away the pith (the soft, white part inside the peel). If white pith is left on, the peel will be bitter. Cut peel into ⅜-inch-wide strips. Wrap and refrigerate the peeled fruit for another use.

In a 2-quart saucepan combine 1⅓ cups sugar and ⅓ cup water. Cover and bring to boiling. Add orange peel strips. Return to boiling, stirring constantly to dissolve sugar. Reduce heat. Cook, uncovered, over medium-low heat. Mixture should boil at a moderate, steady rate over entire surface. Cook, stirring occasionally, for 15 minutes or until peel is almost translucent. Remove from heat.

Using a slotted spoon, remove peel from syrup, allowing each spoonful to drain over the saucepan about 30 seconds. Transfer peel to a wire rack set over waxed paper. Set cooked peel aside until cool enough to handle but still warm and slightly sticky. Roll peel in additional sugar to coat. Continue drying on the rack for 1 to 2 hours. Store, tightly covered, in a cool, dry place for up to 1 week or in freezer for up to 6 months.

Dark Chocolate-Orange Glaze: In a heavy small saucepan bring 3 tablespoons whipping cream to a simmer over medium heat. Remove from heat. Stir in ⅓ cup finely chopped dark chocolate and ⅛ teaspoon orange extract until chocolate is melted. Cool 5 minutes before using.

Fudge Brownie Tassies
Shown on page 125

- ½ cup butter, softened
- 1 3-ounce package cream cheese, softened
- 1 cup all-purpose flour
- ½ cup semisweet chocolate pieces
- 2 tablespoons butter
- ⅓ cup sugar
- 1 egg, lightly beaten
- 1 teaspoon vanilla
- 24 Macadamia nuts, hazelnuts (filberts), almonds, or walnut pieces
- 1 recipe Chocolate Butter Frosting

1. For pastry, in a medium mixing bowl beat the ½ cup butter and cream cheese with an electric mixer on medium to high speed for 30 seconds. Using a wooden spoon, stir in flour. Cover and chill dough about 1 hour or until easy to handle.

2. Preheat oven to 325°F. Shape dough into 24 balls. Press each ball evenly onto the bottom and up the sides of ungreased 1¾-inch muffin cups.

3. For filling, in a small saucepan combine chocolate pieces and the 2 tablespoons butter; stir over low heat until melted. Remove from heat. Stir in sugar, egg, and vanilla. Place a nut and about 1½ teaspoons of the chocolate mixture into each dough-lined muffin cup.

4. Bake for 20 to 25 minutes or until pastry is golden and filling is puffed. Cool tassies in muffin cups on wire racks for 5 minutes. Carefully remove tassies from pans by running a knife around the edge of each cup. Transfer to wire racks and let cool.

5. Pipe or spoon Chocolate Butter Frosting onto tassies. If desired, top with additional nuts. Makes 24 tassies.

Chocolate Butter Frosting: In a medium mixing bowl beat 2 tablespoons softened butter with an electric mixer on medium to high speed until smooth. Beat in 2 tablespoons unsweetened cocoa powder. Gradually add ¼ cup powdered sugar, beating well. Slowly beat in 1 tablespoon milk and ½ teaspoon vanilla. Gradually beat in 1¼ cups powdered sugar. Beat in

enough additional milk, 1 teaspoon at a time, to reach piping consistency.

To store: Prepare tassies as directed through step 4. Place cooled tassies in a single layer in an airtight container. Cover and store in the refrigerator for up to 3 days or freeze for up to 3 months. Before serving, thaw tassies, if frozen, and pipe or spoon on frosting.

Chocolate-Peppermint Pie
Shown on page 126

- 1¼ cups all-purpose flour
- ¼ teaspoon salt
- 3 tablespoons shortening
- 2 tablespoons butter
- 4 to 5 tablespoons cold water

¾ cup sugar

¼ cup cornstarch

3 cups milk

5 egg yolks, lightly beaten

1 tablespoon butter

2 teaspoons vanilla

2 ounces unsweetened chocolate, chopped

2 ounces white chocolate, chopped

⅛ teaspoon peppermint extract

1 recipe Sweetened Whipped Cream
   Dark chocolate curls
   Striped round peppermint candies, coarsely crushed

1. Preheat oven to 450°F. For crust, in a medium bowl stir together flour and salt. Using a pastry blender, cut in shortening and the 2 tablespoons butter until pieces are pea-size. Sprinkle 1 tablespoon of the water over part of the flour mixture; gently toss with a fork. Push moistened pastry to the side of the bowl. Repeat moistening flour mixture, using 1 tablespoon of the water at a time, until all the flour mixture is moistened. Form pastry into a ball.

2. On a lightly floured surface, flatten dough ball. Roll dough from center to edges, forming a 12-inch circle. Transfer to a 9-inch pie plate; avoid stretching. Gently press into plate. Trim pastry to ½ inch beyond edge of pie plate. Fold under extra pastry. Crimp edge as desired. Prick bottom and sides of pastry with a fork. Line pastry with a double thickness of foil. Bake pastry for 8 minutes. Remove foil; bake for 5 to 6 minutes more or until crust is golden. Cool on a wire rack.

3. For filling, in a medium saucepan combine sugar and cornstarch. Gradually stir in milk. Cook and stir over medium-high heat until thickened and bubbly; reduce heat. Cook and stir for 2 minutes more. Remove from heat. Gradually stir about 1 cup of the hot filling into yolks. Add egg yolk mixture to saucepan. Bring to a gentle boil; reduce heat. Cook and stir for 2 minutes. Remove from heat. Stir in 1 tablespoon butter and vanilla. Divide hot filling between two bowls. Quickly whisk the unsweetened chocolate into one bowl until melted and smooth. Whisk the white chocolate and peppermint extract into other bowl until melted and smooth.

4. Immediately spoon the two fillings in alternate mounds into the baked pastry shell. Use a thin metal spatula to gently swirl the two puddings together to marble. Cover surface of filling with plastic wrap. Chill for 4 to 24 hours before serving.

5. To serve, spoon or pipe Sweetened Whipped Cream on top of pie. Top with chocolate curls and sprinkle with crushed peppermint candies. Makes 8 servings.

Sweetened Whipped Cream: In a chilled medium mixing bowl beat 1 cup whipping cream, 2 tablespoons sugar, and ½ teaspoon vanilla with the chilled beaters of an electric mixer on medium speed until soft peaks form.

Chocolate-Mint Ice Cream

Shown on page 126

1 quart half-and-half or light cream (4 cups)

2 cups milk

1½ cups coarsely chopped fresh mint leaves

2 cups sugar

⅔ cup unsweetened cocoa powder

¼ cup all-purpose flour

¼ teaspoon salt

2 eggs, lightly beaten

1 cup whipping cream

1 tablespoon vanilla

3 ounces white baking chocolate (optional)

1 teaspoon shortening (optional)
   Fresh raspberries (optional)
   Fresh mint sprigs (optional)

1. In a large saucepan bring half-and-half, milk, and 1½ cups mint leaves to boiling over medium heat. Remove pan from heat. Cover and let stand 30 minutes. Strain liquid through a fine sieve into a bowl, pressing mint leaves with the back of a spoon. Discard the mint leaves.

2. In the same saucepan combine sugar, cocoa powder, flour, and salt; stir in strained milk mixture and eggs. Cook over medium heat, stirring constantly, until mixture just boils. Reduce heat; cook and stir 1 minute more. Remove from heat. Whisk in whipping cream and vanilla. Transfer to a large bowl; cover and chill thoroughly.

3. Freeze in a 4- to 5-quart ice cream freezer according to manufacturer's directions. Ripen for 4 hours.*

4. If desired, in a small saucepan combine white chocolate and shortening. Cook and stir over medium-low heat until chocolate is melted and smooth. Drizzle over ice cream in serving bowls. If desired, garnish with raspberries and mint sprigs. Makes 2½ quarts (twenty ½-cup servings).

*Test Kitchen Tip: To ripen ice cream made in a traditional-style ice cream freezer, after churning, remove the lid and dasher and cover the top with waxed paper or foil. Plug the lid's hole with cloth, then replace the lid on the can. Fill the outer freezer bucket with ice and rock salt—enough to cover the top of the freezer can—in a ratio of 4 cups ice to 1 cup rock salt. Let stand at room temperature about 4 hours. (To ripen ice cream made in an ice cream freezer with an insulated freezer bowl, transfer the ice cream to a freezer-proof container. Cover and store in the freezer for 4 hours or according to manufacturer's directions.)

colors
of christmas

Choose the colors you love to set the stage for a most wonderful holiday.

Combine the colors of Christmas in a **Full-of-Color Holiday Wreath**, *opposite*, that showcases vintage lights and colorful accents. Fill a glass ball ornament with tiny trims to make a **Playful Christmas Trim**, *above*. The little ornaments cluster together to add multicolor sparkle to any tree. Instructions are on page 142.

Make clever **Wreaths in Red and Green**, *right*, with simple components that work up quickly. Velvet ribbon is the theme on the ribbon wreath and candy canes are the focus on the wreath in red and white. The wreaths are made using plastic foam bases with a pretty ribbon to complete each wreath. Instructions are on page 142.

Create some holiday shimmer with floating candles. Assembling these **Shimmering Candles**, *above*, is accomplished in just a few minutes yet the result is impressive. Instructions are on pages 142–143.

Let the snow outside be your inspiration for a **Winter White Mantel,** *opposite*. All decked out with star-studded mini trees and boughs of snow-covered greenery, the arrangement is completed by adding a pair of white ice skates.

Pile up snowballs that last from season to season when you create a **Sparkling Snowball Centerpiece,** *above,* using plastic foam balls and pure white wax. Instructions are on page 143.

Let the colors of gold and silver make your holiday sparkle. Create a **Decoupage Fabric Star**, *opposite top*, that is easily constructed using little pieces of fabric and decoupage medium. Layer favorite metallics of gold and silver in an **Ornamental Pitcher**, *opposite below*, that is used as a centerpiece or anywhere you need a touch of sparkle. Snowflakes are dressed for the holidays in a **Quilted Snowflake Table Runner**, *above*, that is stitched with metallic threads. Instructions are on pages 143–145.

Create beautifully blue decorations for this year's holiday. Start with a shiny **Holiday Beaded Tree**, *opposite*, using all kinds of holiday sparkle. Simply pin sequins, Christmas balls, and other glittery shapes to a purchased foam cone. Twigs and lots and lots of glittery color make a lovely **Sky-Blue Glitter Wreath**, *top left*. Crisp and clean as the winter sky, **See-Through Snowflakes**, *left*, combine two types of fabric for transparent appeal. Instructions are on pages 145–147.

Full-of-Color Holiday Wreath
Shown on page 133

WHAT YOU NEED
Fresh evergreen wreath
Vintage (or reproduction) large-bulb
    string of lights; beaded berries
Fine wire
Ornaments in multiple colors
2½-inch-wide polka dot ribbon
Scissors
Spray snow

HERE'S HOW
Wrap the lights around the wreath and
secure with wire. **Note:** The lights are
used for ornamentation only—they will
not be lit. Wire the ornaments onto the
wreath as desired. Tie a large bow and
wire to the top of the wreath. Spray
lightly with snow. Let dry. Add a wire
to the back for hanging.

Playful Christmas Trim
Shown on page 132

WHAT YOU NEED
Large clear glass ornament with
    removable top
Small ornaments to fit into
    glass ornament
Narrow ribbon

HERE'S HOW
Be sure the clear ornament is clean and
dry. Remove the top and put the smaller
ornaments into the ball. Replace the top
and add the ribbon.

Wreaths in Red and Green
Shown on page 134

**WHAT YOU NEED FOR THE
CANDY CANE WREATH**
Plastic foam wreath form
White satin ribbon
Hot glue gun and glue sticks
Mini candy canes
Small red ornaments
Red and red-and-white striped ribbon
Scissors; stapler

HERE'S HOW
Wrap wreath form with white satin
ribbon. Layer on the candy canes
randomly, hot-gluing them in place.
Hot-glue red ornaments on top of the
candy canes. Fashion a bow from three
lengths of ribbon shaped into
progressively smaller loops. Stack the
ribbon loops and staple them at the
center. Wrap with another piece of
ribbon around all three, and hot-glue a
pair of tails to the back before affixing to
the bottom of the wreath with hot glue.

**WHAT YOU NEED FOR THE
RIBBON WREATH**
Plastic foam wreath form
Velvet, satin, and taffeta ribbon in
    shades of green
Florist's wire; scissors
Florist's picks
White ornaments
Hot-glue gun and glue sticks

HERE'S HOW
Cut lengths of velvet, satin, and taffeta
ribbons. Fold the ribbon into loops, and
wire several loops onto a florist's pick.

Cover the surface of the plastic foam
wreath form with the ribbons, alternating
ribbon types, shades, and heights for
optimal interest. Nestle white ornaments
between the loops and hot-glue them in
place. Make the finishing bow by layering
velvet ribbon loops onto a longer piece of
ribbon and hot-gluing them in place.
Wire the bow to a pick and anchor it to
the wreath bottom.

Shimmering Candles
Shown on page 135

WHAT YOU NEED
Goblets or small dishes in red and green
Tray (optional)
Water
Floating candles
Sequins or beads
Ornaments (optional)

HERE'S HOW

Be sure the dishes are clean and dry. Arrange on a tray if desired. Fill the dishes two-thirds full with water. Add the floating candles. Add beads or sequins to the water. Light the candles. Nestle ornaments around the base of the dishes. *Never leave a burning candle unattended.*

Winter White Mantel

Shown on page 136

WHAT YOU NEED

Fresh cedar branches
Purchased acrylic snowflakes and
    other snow-related items
Spray snow
White vintage ice skates
Purchased glass icicle ornaments

HERE'S HOW

Flock the purchased snowflakes and other items by spraying them with spray snow.

Allow to dry. Set aside. Heap mounds of fresh-cut cedar branches on a mantel. Add the snowed items and spray the cedar branches lightly. Securely hang ice skates from the display. Add the dangling glass icicle ornaments.

Sparkling Snowball Centerpiece

Shown on page 137

WHAT YOU NEED

Paraffin wax; knife
Clean old tin can big enough for the
    ball to fit into
Old pan big enough to hold the tin can
Water; stove or hot plate
Skewer
Round plastic foam balls, such as
    Styrofoam
Bowl of cold water; waxed paper
Fine white glitter

HERE'S HOW

1. Cut up the wax and place in the old tin can. Place the tin can in an old pan filled half-full of water and place on low heat on a hot plate or stove. Watch the wax carefully and just melt the wax. Remove from heat. **Note:** If the wax gets too hot it can explode—watch it carefully. **2.** Skewer the foam ball and dip into the melted wax. Immediately dip the waxed ball into the cold water in the bowl. Then dip the ball in the wax again, then back to the cold water until the ball is entirely covered. While the waxed ball is still hot, sprinkle with glitter. Lay on the waxed paper to dry. Stack the waxed balls in a round dish for the centerpiece.

Decoupaged Fabric Star

Shown on page 138

WHAT YOU NEED

⅛ yard of silver or gold tone-on-tone
    cotton fabric
Scissors
3-D cardboard star shape (available at
    crafts stores)
White glue
Water
Disposable plastic bowl
Small craft paint brush
Waxed paper
Fine iridescent silver or gold glitter

HERE'S HOW

1. Cut the fabric into about 1-inch squares. In the small bowl mix equal parts of white glue and water. Working over a piece of waxed paper, dip several pieces of fabric in the glue mixture and place onto the cardboard shape, overlapping edges of fabric to completely cover the cardboard.

2. Press down fabric corners and smooth with wet finger. Use paintbrush to brush over the pieces with more of the glue and water mixture. Work on a small section at a time. Clipping fabric at the points will help wrap the fabric around these areas. When one side is covered, carefully turn the shape over and complete the other side. Allow glue to dry.

3. Brush a thin mixture of the glue and water mixture over one side of the shape and lightly sprinkle with fine glitter. Repeat for other side. Allow to dry.

Ornamental Pitcher
Shown on page 138

WHAT YOU NEED
Clear glass pitcher
Small ornaments in metallic colors
Wooden skewer

HERE'S HOW
Be sure the pitcher is clean and dry. Place the ornaments in the pitcher layering alternate colors and using the skewer as needed. Use at least 3 inches of one color before changing colors for maximum effect.

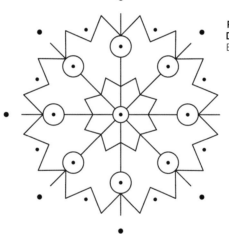

TABLE RUNNER DESIGNS
Enlarge at 200%

Quilted Snowflake Table Runner
Shown on page 139

WHAT YOU NEED
Tracing paper or copier; pencil
⅝ yard ivory double foil cotton fabric
¼ yard gold mesh fabric
¼ yard silver lamé fabric
Scrap of gold lamé fabric
Marking pen; scissors; ruler
Stabilizer or thin paper
Metallic sewing machine needle
Matching sewing thread
Gold metallic sewing thread
Silver metallic sewing thread
Thin cotton batting (about 12×44 inches)
3-mm and 4-mm iridescent jewels
Jewel glue

HERE'S HOW
1. Enlarge and trace or copy snowflake designs, *above*. Set aside. Cut five 8×8-inch blocks (to be trimmed to 6½×6½ inches later) from ivory fabric. Cut six 2½×6½-inch pieces from ivory fabric and the same from gold mesh fabric. Cut two 2½×38½-inch strips from both ivory and gold mesh fabric. Cut four 2½-inch squares from gold lamé fabric. Cut two ¾×38½-inch strips and two ¾×7-inch strips from silver lamé fabric. Cut one 11½×44-inch piece from ivory fabric for the backing. Cut three 2½-inch-wide strips from silver lamé fabric for the binding.

2. With marking pen, mark snowflake designs onto center of 8-inch squares of ivory fabric. Stitch snowflake designs with gold and silver metallic threads, using decorative, small zigzag, and straight stitches to sew around lines of design. **Note:** It is helpful to use a metallic sewing machine needle and stabilizer or thin paper on the back of the design. Trim blocks to 6½-inch squares. Lay gold mesh fabric on top of ivory fabric strips; baste around outside edges. Using ¼-inch seams for all stitching, sew the five snowflake blocks together with four strips of 2½×6½-inch ivory and gold mesh sashings.

3. Fold wrong sides together of the ¾-inch-wide strips of silver lamé fabric. Press carefully (use a press cloth to eliminate melting of metallic fabrics). Baste narrow silver strips to long sides of center blocks and sashing strips. Sew narrow silver strips to short ends, folding under raw edges at ends. Stitch gold lamé squares to ends of two remaining 2½×6½-inch ivory and gold mesh strips. Stitch long borders to top and bottom of blocks. Stitch side borders with gold squares to ends.

4. Layer top, batting, and backing and quilt as desired. Sew silver binding to outside edges. Glue jewels to snowflake blocks at dots indicated on pattern, using a variety of sizes.

Holiday Beaded Tree
Shown on page 140

WHAT YOU NEED
3⅞×8⅞-inch plastic foam cone such as Styrofoam
Package of 100 long pearlized straight pins
Multicolor glitter craft paint and paintbrush
5 silver glittered leaf floral picks
1 teal color bead grape floral pick
Assorted teal, blue, and silver sequins
White and teal snowflake-shaped foam stickers
Crafts glue; scissors
Iridescent teal star topper
Clear glass votive cup

HERE'S HOW

1. Paint the plastic cone with the craft paint and let dry. Cut silver metallic leaves from floral picks and separate into large, medium, and smaller sizes. Insert a pearlized pin into a single large leaf and poke into the cone at the bottom, placing at a diagonal.

2. Continue to place single leaves at an angle to make a row around the bottom of the cone. Arrange leaves in groups of three with larger leaves at the bottom of the cone, medium-size at the center, and the smallest ones toward the top of the cone. Poke a pearlized pin through the group of three and fan them out to cover as much of the cone as possible.

3. Cut teal-color beads from the grape cluster floral pick. Leave about 1 inch of wire extending from each bead. Poke beads into cone at areas where leaf clusters are placed. Continue to fill in spaces.

4. Using crafts glue fill in any remaining areas with additional pieces of silver foliage from the floral picks. Poke star topper into top of cone using wire from topper, or glue in place with craft glue.

5. Turn clear glass votive upside down and spread a thick layer of crafts glue on flat bottom. Place decorated tree on top of votive; let dry.

Sky-Blue Glitter Wreath
Shown on page 141

WHAT YOU NEED
6-inch wooden craft ring
Blue glitter paint
Paintbrush; scissors
Artificial leaf vine rope
Hot-glue gun and glue sticks

HERE'S HOW
Paint the wooden craft ring with glitter paint and allow to dry. Wrap vine rope around outside edge of ring and cut at length desired. Hot-glue the vine to the ring. Make additional rows of vine to spiral around the ring, gluing as you go. Clip apart and glue small sections to fill in around the ring.

See-Through Snowflakes
Shown on page 141

WHAT YOU NEED
Tracing paper or copier
Pencil
Scissors; straight pins
Heavy iron-on interfacing
6×12-inch piece of woven white or
    light blue fabric (for 1 snowflake)
Sheer iridescent glittery fabrics
Fabric glue
Glittery silver and iridescent white
    fabric paints
Awl
Narrow silver, blue and white ribbon
    or cording

HERE'S HOW
1. Trace or copy patterns, *below,* and
cut out both snowflake and star patterns
individually. Set aside.
2. Fuse interfacing onto the back of
woven fabrics to be used for outside of
snowflakes. Fold interfaced fabric in half
with right sides together, pin snowflake
pattern onto interfaced side and trace
snowflake pattern onto the back of the
interfacing. Cut through both layers of
fabric to make two snowflake shapes for
each ornament. Leave snowflake shapes
pinned together. Trace and cut out star
pattern. Trace around star pattern in
center of double layer of snowflake shape.
Carefully cut the star shape from
the center of the snowflake.
3. Cut a piece of iridescent fabric slightly
larger than the star shape. Using fabric
glue make a line of glue around the star
outline and position sheer fabric on top of
the interfaced side of one snowflake shape.
Make a thin line of glue around the sheer
fabric and over all the interfaced sides of
the snowflake. Place the other snowflake
on top, interfaced sides together to
sandwich the sheer fabric inside the
two snowflake shapes. Press the layers
together to lie flat.
4. On the front side of the ornament,
edge both star shape and snowflake shape
with silver glitter or white iridescent fabric
paint. Allow paint to dry; poke a hole in
one edge. Cut a length of ribbon or
cording, poke through the hole in the
snowflake, and tie a knot through the end
to hang the ornament.

SEE-THROUGH
SNOWFLAKES
Full-Size Pattern

*Make your holiday cozy and warm
with candles in all styles and colors.*

holiday glow

White pearl beads nestle around a warm candle to create

Beaded Candlelight, *above.* For **Winter Warmth,**

opposite, casually dress a mantel with pepperberries and

lacy greenery. Then introduce a little razzle-dazzle with blue

candles on the mantel and a grouping of candles in the

fireplace opening. Instructions are on page 156.

Castaway sweater fabrics become warm and **Cozy Candleholders,** *above,* when they are slipped over glass votive containers. The freshness of greenery and the welcoming warmth of candlelight combine to make **Greenery Candles,** *opposite top.*

Core bright red apples, slide in a votive candle, and add a basil leaf to make **Apple and Basil Candles,** *opposite bottom.* Set a trio of apples on a simple plate and enjoy the pretty red and green combination. Instructions are on pages 156–157.

Feature the twinkle of simple holiday candles by using a picture frame as a base for **Framed Flames,** *opposite.* The glass of the picture frame reflects the glowing candles. Pretty buttons all in creamy white surround a beeswax candle to make a **Country Candle,** *above,* that adds a cozy feel to the holiday table. Instructions are on pages 157–158.

Line the walkway with dozens of **Canning Jar Luminarias**, *right,* to light the way for your guests on Christmas Eve. Use old-fashioned blue canning jars or purchase new jars at any grocery store.

Tied together in holiday style, this **Beribboned Trio**, *opposite,* is simple to make and lights up the holiday table with pretty candlelight.

Use a linoleum cutter to carve a simple design into a pillar candle. Then surround the **Clever Carved Candle**, *right,* with individual Christmas replacement lights. Instructions are on page 158.

Beaded Candlelight

Shown on page 148

WHAT YOU NEED

Small hurricane-style glass candleholder
White candle
Package of white pearl beads
   (available at crafts stores)

HERE'S HOW

Be sure the glass is clean and dry. Set the candle in the container. Pour the pearl beads around the candle. Adjust the candle as necessary. *Never leave a burning candle unattended.*

Winter Warmth

Shown on page 149

WHAT YOU NEED

Greenery; pepperberries
Blue candles
Potted small trees
White candles in various sizes

HERE'S HOW

Arrange the greenery, pepperberries, and candles on the mantel. Add a potted tree at each end. Place the white candles inside the fireplace opening, arranging them at different heights. *Never leave a burning candle unattended.*

Cozy Candleholders

Shown on page 150

WHAT YOU NEED

Recycled jars (any size and shape)
   or purchased votives in
   glass containers
Felt scraps
Marking pen; scissors
Discarded sweaters
Matching sewing thread
Needle
Fabric glue
Coordinating color yarn
Candles to fit inside recycled jars
Jingle bell (optional)

HERE'S HOW

1. Trace around bottom of the jars onto a scrap of felt and cut shapes out just inside marking lines. This will be used to finish the bottom of the candles. Set aside.
2. Cut sweaters into rectangle shapes large enough to wrap around the jars and extend at least 1 inch longer than the height of the containers. Be sure to plan to have a finished edge at the top of the jars and consider whether you plan to roll a cuff over at the top when you decide the length of the sweater piece. Sleeves and bottom ribbed edges of sweaters work nicely for the top finished edge. Some sleeves may be just the width needed to slide over the jar. If cutting from a larger section of the sweater, cut the size needed, place right sides together and stitch a narrow ¼-seam, by hand or machine, down the length of the piece. Turn right side out and insert jars into created tubes. Turn the jars upside down. Using a double strand of sewing thread, sew around the cut edge of the sweaters using large basting stitches to gather edges together around the bottom of the jars. Knot ends to secure.
3. Glue felt shapes onto bottoms of jars over gathered sweater edges. Turn jars upright and embellish with crocheted yarn tie, and if desired, a jingle bell hanging from single yarn. Put candles into the jars. *Never leave a burning candle unattended.*

A

B

C

Greenery Candles
Shown on page 151

WHAT YOU NEED
Tall clear glass container
Flat evergreen pieces
Spray adhesive
Sturdy scissors or floral snips
Candle to fit inside container

HERE'S HOW
1. Prepare the glass surface by cleaning
with window cleaner. Select any flat
evergreen pieces. Coat the greenery with
spray adhesive. See photo A, *top left*.
2. Wait a few seconds for the adhesive
to get tacky and then attach each piece
to the outside of the container with the
ends hanging from the bottom of the
container and tops at random heights.
See photo B, *middle left*.
3. Allow the greenery to dry for a few
minutes. Then trim the bottoms with
sturdy scissors, floral snips, or garden shears.
Place the candle into the container.
See Photo C, *lower below. Never leave
a burning candle unattended.*

Apple and Basil Candles
Shown on page 151

WHAT YOU NEED
Fresh red apples
Apple corer
Sharp knife
Votive in glass container

Large basil leaf
Clear glass plate
Small bits of greenery

HERE'S HOW
Wash and dry the apples. Slice off the
bottoms slightly if necessary to ensure
that the apple sits level. Use the corer to
core the apple. Use a knife if necessary to
create an opening large enough to hold
the glass votive container. Tuck basil
leaves between the glass and the apples.
Set on a glass plate. Add bits of greenery.
Never leave a burning candle unattended.

Framed Flames
Shown on page 152

WHAT YOU NEED
Picture frame with glass in desired style
Piece of patterned scrapbook paper to
    fit inside the frame
Candles in desired heights
Small ornaments in colors to match or
    coordinate with candle

HERE'S HOW
Measure the frame and cut a piece of
patterned scrapbook paper to fit inside it.
Place paper in frame. Turn over and
arrange candles and ornaments on top of
the framed paper. *Never leave a burning
candle unattended.*

Country Candle

Shown on page 153

WHAT YOU NEED
Small clear glass dish
White or cream-color pillar-style
    beeswax candle
Small white or cream vintage or
    new buttons in a variety of shapes
    and sizes

HERE'S HOW
Be sure the dish is clean and dry. Center
the candle in the dish. Fill the dish with
buttons arranging them as desired around
the candle. *Never leave a burning candle
unattended.*

Canning Jar Luminarias

Shown on page 154

WHAT YOU NEED
Vintage or new canning jars
Water
Red wire-edge ribbon
Floating candles
Glitter (optional)

HERE'S HOW
Wash and dry the jars. Fill two-thirds full
with water. Tie a ribbon around the top of
the jar. Carefully add the candle to the
water. Add glitter if desired.

Clever Carved Candle

Shown on page 154

WHAT YOU NEED
Pillar candle in desired color
Pencil
Linoleum cutter with blades
Small paintbrush
Small glass plate
Individual replacement
    Christmas lightbulbs

HERE'S HOW
Wipe off the candle and mark a simple
design with the pencil or carve the design
freehand. Choose a blade that fits the
design and place in the cutter holder.
Working away from hands and face,
carve the design into the candle. Use
the paintbrush to brush away the carved
wax that may stick into the design.
Place the candle on the plate and
surround with lightbulbs. *Never leave
a burning candle unattended.*

Beribboned Trio

Shown on page 155

WHAT YOU NEED
3 votive candles in
    glass containers
1 yard of 2-inch-wide patterned ribbon
Pencil
Needle; thread
Scissors

HERE'S HOW
Set the votives in a row. Fold the ribbon
in half. Put the folded edge at one end of
the row. Pull the ribbon around the first
votive and mark the point on the ribbon
with a pencil. Repeat for the other two
candles. Thread the needle and stitch
across the pencil lines between candles
one and two and two and three using a
running stitch securing at both beginning
and end. Pull the ribbon around last
votive end and tie it into a bow. Trim
ends of ribbon.

index

Sources

Candy
Hammond's Candies
hammondscandies.com

Ribbon
hancockfabrics.com
joannfabrics.com

Michaels
michaels.com

Hobby Lobby
hobbylobby.com

Scrapbooking Supplies
Bazzill
bazzillbasics.com

EK Success
eksuccess.com

Making Memories
makingmemories.com

My Mind's Eye
mymindseye.com

Breakfast Goodie Jar Recipes

Chocolate Chunk Pecan Muffins

To put in jar
1¾ cups all-purpose flour
½ cup sugar
2 teaspoons baking powder
¼ teaspoon salt
½ cup chocolate chunks
½ cup chopped pecans

To write on card
Grease twelve 2½-inch muffin cups or line with paper bake cups:
set side. Empty contents of jar into a medium bowl. Make a well
in center of flour mixture. Combine 1 beaten egg, ¾ cup milk,
and ¼ cup cooking oil. Add egg mixture all at once to flour
mixture. Stir just until moistened (batter should be lumpy).
Spoon batter into prepared muffin cups, filling each two-thirds
full. Bake in a 400°F oven for 18 to 20 minutes or until golden
and a wooden toothpick inserted in centers comes out clean.
Cool in muffin cups on a wire rack for 5 minutes. Remove from
muffin cups; serve warm. Makes 12 muffins.

Breakfast Cornbread

To put in jar
1 cup all-purpose flour
¾ cup cornmeal
2 to 3 tablespoons sugar
2½ teaspoons baking powder
¾ teaspoon salt

To write on card
Grease twelve 2½-inch muffin cups or line with paper bake cups:
set side. Empty contents of jar into medium-size mixing bowl.
Make a well in the center of flour mixture. Combine 2 beaten
eggs, 1 cup milk, and ¼ cup oil. Add egg mixture to flour
mixture. Stir until just moistened. Pour batter into prepared
muffin cups. Bake for 10 to 15 minutes in a 400°F oven until a
wooden toothpick inserted near center comes out clean. Cool
on wire rack, serve warm. Makes 12 muffins.

Breakfast Oatmeal Mix

To put in jar
2¾ cups old-fashioned oatmeal
¼ cup dried cranberries
2 tablespoons sugar

To write on card
For one serving, mix ¾ cup mixture and ¾ cup milk.
Heat in microwave for 3 minutes stirring as needed.
Serve immediately.

Stitch Diagrams

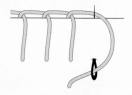

Blanket Stitch

Buttonhole Stitch

Chain Stitch

Fern Stitch

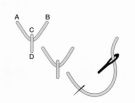

Fly Stitch

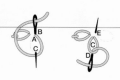

Lazy Daisy Stitch

Stem Stitch

Knitting Abbreviations

approx	approximately
beg	begin(ning)(s)
cn	cable needle
dec	decrease(s)(ing)
end	ending
est	established
inc	increase(s)(ing)
k or K	knit
p or P	purl
pat	pattern
pwise	as if to purl
rem	remain(s)(ing)
rep	repeat(s)(ing)
rev	reverse
RS	right side(s) of work
sl	slip
sm	slip marker
st(s)	stitch(es)
St st	stockinette stitch
tbl	through the back loop(s)
tog	together
WS	wrong side(s) of work
yo	yarn over
yon	yarn over needle
yrn	yarn around needle
[ ]	work step in brackets the number of times indicated
( )	work instructions within parentheses in the place directed and the number of times indicated
*	repeat the instructions following the single asterisk as directed

To Felt Wool or Wool Garments
Garment or wool must
be at least 80% wool to
felt properly. Wash
garment or wool in hot
water in washing
mashine. Dry in hot
dryer. Press if desired.